Jesus in the Shadows

Seeing Jesus in the Bible's most well-known Old Testament stories

by

Eric Robinson

To Gina:

*For the woman who would rather talk about
the Bible than fashion, shopping, decorating, or even sports
(or anything else for that matter);
God gave me the perfect match. I'm indebted to you
for your godly insights that spur me on. I love you.*

Endorsements

From the moment the first chapter of this off-the-hook book begins, "What if Jesus led a Bible study?" I was hooked. You will be too. Hear the Jesus story as it should be told, from Genesis to Revelation.
    Leonard Sweet, best-selling author and professor, chief contributor to sermons.com

This is a highly readable book, written to be understood by everyone, showing how the Jesus story permeates all the Scriptures. The chapters enable the reader to see how the entire Bible was meant to prepare for Christ, and I recommend it highly.
    Grant Osborne, author of* The Hermeneutical Spiral*

Eric Robinson presents a stunning portrait of Christ throughout the ages. I was blown away, again and again, by the insights on every page. If you've ever wondered how the Old and New Testaments fit together, read this book. You'll discover JESUS in all His glory, just as God painted Him for us, on the canvas of human history.
    Dr. Andrew Farley, bestselling author of* The Naked Gospel *and* God Without Religion

Eric Robinson has written a wonderfully insightful study from the Hebrew Scriptures, showing how they point to Y'shua ha Mashiach, Jesus the Messiah. In a day when stories are becoming more and more important as vehicles for communicating truth, this book is a great reminder how God has woven the promise of a redeemer throughout His revelation to Israel. If you love to study the Bible you will gain fresh insight into the eternal purposes of God through reading this refreshing book.
David Brickner, Executive Director of Jews for Jesus, author of *Christ in the Feast of Pentecost*

Table of Contents

Introduction... 1

Chapter 1 If Jesus Led a Bible Study.................... 3

Chapter 2 Second Only to the King
          (Daniel in the Lions' Den)...................... 12

Chapter 3 Unswerving Trust
          (The Sacrifice of Isaac) 24

Chapter 4 Make Mine on the Rocks
          (Moses Strikes the Rock) 33

Chapter 5 Outmatched
          (David and Goliath) 48

Chapter 6 Because I Said So
          (Jonah and the Whale) 61

Chapter 7 Stuck in a Well
          (Joseph and His Brothers) 75

Chapter 8 Pinhole Camera
          (Moses on the Mountain with God)............ 88

Chapter 9 Coffee With God 107

Endnotes... 126

Introduction

I hope you love the Bible. I hope you want to understand it better. I hope that the very idea of deepening your relationship with God through Bible study is something that sounds exciting to you. But whether it is or not, get ready to do just that. Get ready to know Him through His Word in an incredible and powerful way. You will not be able to help being transformed.

The way of looking at the Scripture put forth in this book dates back to an ancient Jewish culture that understood much more, as a whole, than we do about hearing God speak through His Word. Although the church used this kind of interpretive practice for over sixteen hundred years, with the beginning of the Enlightenment and the rise of the modern era it began to die out until it is now comparatively almost non-existent. During the time it was being pushed out of the church because it did not fit with a scientific approach to research, the leader of a Bible school in Scotland, Patrick Fairbairn, wrote about what he believed to be a terrible injustice to the proper understanding of God's Word. He wrote in the middle of the 1800s so the quote is a bit difficult to understand on first read, but I will interpret in plain language following the excerpt.

Jesus in the Shadows

"Were men accustomed, as they should be, to search for the germs of Christian truth in the earliest Scriptures, and to regard the inspired records of both covenants as having for their leading object 'the testimony of Jesus,' they would know how much they were losers by such an undue contraction of the typical element in the Old Testament Scripture. And in proportion as a more profound and spiritual acquaintance with the divine word is cultivated, will the feeling of dissatisfaction grow in respect to a style of interpretation that so miserably dwarfs and cripples the relation which the preparatory bears to the ultimate in God's revelations."[1]

In simple words, it means if people were used to seeing just how much the Jesus story fills the entire Bible they would quickly recognize how terribly inadequate any kind of interpretation is that does not do so. It is my favorite quote to show why we must retrain our minds to approach Scripture this way—the way the apostles did. Simply put, we are missing out. But the great part is we can stop missing out. We really can learn to allow the Holy Spirit to show Jesus to us in *ALL* the Scriptures. It is what we are made to do . . . put Him first.

So enough introduction already . . . time to get started.

Chapter 1

If Jesus Led a Bible Study . . .

What if Jesus led a Bible study? That is such a great question, isn't it? What would it be like if Jesus led a great, in-depth Bible study? What would He focus on? Where would He take us in God's Word and what points would He make?

Of course, the answers to these questions would be dictated by the audience Jesus had. He would reach those who were present exactly where they would benefit most. Actually, we have an example of this very thing in the New Testament (several examples, really, if you consider Jesus' overall use of Scripture). Let's look at what is going on in Luke 24.

At the end of Luke, the disciples that have followed Jesus for so long and have pinned all their hopes on Him as Israel's Messiah have basically given up on a significant change in their lives or in Israel's future. Jesus, whom they saw as the one to lead Israel to a future that would reflect the glorious era of David and Solomon, has been executed as a criminal. Apparently, even His great power to raise the dead was ineffective in preventing His own demise. There are only the imaginings of what might have been and the sorrowful acceptance of dashed hopes and a status quo future.

Now two former disciples walk the road together, discouraged and mournful, recounting the sad events of the last few days (Luke 24:14). It is at this moment that an unknown figure approaches and begins to walk beside the travelers. As the modern readers, we will soon find out that this is Jesus, Himself, now risen from the dead and more powerful than ever. Wahoo!! But I digress . . .

Before the disciples recognize Jesus as being risen from the dead, something very powerful and "interpretive" happens to them. Jesus asks the disciples what they have been talking about as they walked along. One of them responds in a way that says it seems almost crazy that someone wouldn't know about the topic of discussion since it is the major event of the past week. Then the man quickly gives Jesus the highlights of the past few days (how ironic), culminating in the empty tomb. The two men are obviously perplexed at this entire turn of events. After all, they were so certain, along with many others, that Jesus had to be the Messiah sent from God to rescue the nation from the oppression of evil. But it is the next part that is so telling, to them and to us.

Jesus' first words in response to these men after hearing their account of the executed would-be-Messiah are: "How foolish you are, and how slow to believe all that the prophets have spoken! Did not the Messiah have to suffer these things and then enter His glory?" (Luke 24:25-26).

Now wait just a second. Let's read that a few times just to let it sink in. The men are in a very disheartened state. They have been witness to events that led to the death—the death, mind you—of the man they assumed, according to all signs of power and spoken word, to be the

Messiah sent from God who would change the fortunes of Israel for all time. Now they are called foolish by this stranger on the road because, as he is insinuating, they don't understand the Word of God they have been reading and listening to in the synagogues their entire lives. This man is saying that if they did understand it, they would not be so dismayed because it would be clear to them that the Messiah had to experience this kind of terrible suffering and death before the glorious future could ever come to pass.

(I realize that many of you, at this point, are saying right along with me, "Yes, absolutely!" But hold on and stay with me. We are barely getting into the meat of this thing.)

In the next verse, Jesus, still incognito, launches into what must have been one of the best Bible studies of all time. Luke says, specifically: "And beginning with Moses and all the Prophets, he explained to them what was said in all the Scriptures concerning himself" (Luke 24:27).

Wow! Are you kidding?! How great must it have been to hear from Jesus, Himself, how the story of His life, suffering, and death are told clearly throughout all the Scriptures?! This must have been an incredible and glorious few hours on the road.

What Scriptures Are We Talking About?

Luke says first that Jesus began with "Moses." This was a way of saying He started with the books that were written by Moses—the Torah, or what we know as the first five books of Scripture. Then Jesus continued with "all the Prophets." These books include more than what we refer to as the prophetic books in our Old Testament, but they are all books that are part of our Old Testament Scriptures. And, as if we might not be sure that everything was covered in this exhaustive expository lesson, Luke finishes the sentence by saying that "all the Scriptures" were included in Jesus' self-revelation.

Too often we read over this part of Scripture without actually letting what Luke is saying sink in. Luke is telling us that Jesus used the Old Testament to show them why it was obvious (yes, obvious—remember, He called them "foolish" for not understanding) that the Messiah would have to suffer as they witnessed before He would enter into His glorious messianic reign. In just a short time, these two disciples will recognize Him and will speak to each other about how this teaching caused their "hearts to burn" within them, having the Scriptures opened to them in this way (24:32).

Later in the same chapter, we are told that Jesus appeared to the eleven disciples (twelve minus Judas, of course) and others who were together in the upper room and presented the same kind of teaching. Specifically, it states Jesus "opened their minds so they could understand the Scriptures" and He tells them plainly "This is what is written: The Messiah will suffer and rise from the dead on the third day, and repentance for the forgiveness of sins will be preached in his name to all nations, beginning at Jerusalem. " Really?! The suffering, the dying, the rising from the dead, even the day of the rising, and the subsequent proclamation to all nations—all of this is foretold clearly? Why do we not see it easily, then? This is truly revolutionary teaching.

It is this teaching that the disciples will use to change the world. There was no New Testament in "New Testament times." They scattered throughout the world with only what we refer to as the "Old Testament." For them, the Old Testament was the Bible. And in it was the story of Jesus—over and over and over. That story of the suffering and risen Messiah was told so clearly and repeatedly that the disciples could go into a world of Jews who loved and cherished their sacred Scriptures, and Gentiles who had never heard of God's Word, and convince that world that Jesus was the One Savior of all mankind. They did this with only what we refer to as the "Old Testament." Astonishing.

Is it Possible for Me?

The next question we have is actually pretty easy to guess, right? It is, "Why don't *we* get to know?" Where is our explanation, after all? Let's face it—there are very few Christians around today who could use their Old Testaments alone to make a compelling case that Jesus is the Messiah sent from God to save all mankind.

But what if there was a way to know what Jesus taught the disciples that day? What if there was a way to sit in on that incredible Bible study, hearing just how clear it was that God intended for everything to go just as it did? We could see that God orchestrated events since the beginning of time in such a way that the story of redemption would be foretold clearly and repeatedly. That way when it did take place there could be no denying the certainty of Jesus' Lordship.

I believe this is available to us as Christians. I believe that the story of Jesus, incredibly clear and unmistakable, is one that you and I have the capacity to discern, with the Holy Spirit's guidance, of course (John 14:26). The New Testament is really just an elaboration upon, and a recounting of, the fulfillment of the Old Testament. Now, I don't want to downplay the last twenty-seven books of the greatest Book ever written, but I'm simply saying that the New Testament is without meaning if there is no Old

Testament to form its foundation. In the rhythmically translated words of St. Augustine, "In the Old Testament, the New is concealed; in the New, the Old is revealed."[2]

The Story That Must Come Out

What established Jesus as the Messiah of God? It is not the many signs that He did, wonderful though they were. They were only a part of what helped to show His true nature. Even a resurrection from death would not be enough to convince people throughout time to accept Jesus' messianic identity. (Not that "convincing" is always needed. Most people's roadblocks are not intellectual.) But what if the major events of Jesus' life, death, and resurrection could be shown to be foretold in detail in a systematic way in the sacred Scripture, much of which was recorded over a thousand years prior to Jesus' life on earth? And what if it was told over, and over, and over, and over . . . (continue the "over"s as far as you like)? How could this not change everything?

This is exactly how the disciples were taught by Jesus to understand the Scriptures. It is exactly how the disciples taught the world to which they were sent.

Consider that the Jews loved their Scriptures more than any gift they had ever received from the Lord. They believed their Scriptures, wholeheartedly. They cherished their Scriptures. They watched over, protected, and taught their Scriptures to each Jew with fierce loyalty to the text. It was a divine gift from the very heart of God to His people as His chosen vessels in an otherwise hopeless world. Now ask yourselves: would the Jews have allowed anyone to, for even a moment, come into their places of worship and begin treating the Scriptures with obvious irreverence as they used them to support a personal agenda rather than staying true to the tone and nature intended by God? Surely, many tried—and surely, many were expelled from the synagogue, also. But did any such teaching ever gain enough of a foothold to become a worldwide religion? Certainly not.

But what, then, does that say about Christianity? Paul (and one can only assume many of the other apostles) used the Jewish synagogues as ready-made access points to preach his message. If he had played fast and loose with sacred Scripture, surely the echo of his words would not even have died away before he was summarily thrown out of the synagogue, banished completely if not worse. (Many Jews did try to do this to Paul and other disciples.) But instead, what we see are many, many Jews—even thousands at a time—listening to their own Scriptures being preached in parallel to Jesus' life, ministry, death and resurrection, and being utterly convinced—to the point of facing execution, if necessary—that Jesus is their long-awaited Messiah, the culmination of God's plan in history.

When we see the story of Jesus laid out so clearly and perfectly in the Scriptures, over and over again showing the major points of Jesus' life, death, and resurrection, we are at first stunned at the precision with which God made His plan clear so long before its completion. But then, not long afterward, we become grounded in our faith in a way that would otherwise be almost impossible. We realize that Jesus' words, deeds, and the events which surround His life were ordained thousands of years before His earthly existence. This causes our faith to peak at a height that is virtually untouchable by any unbiblical or opposing argument.

This is our goal—the strengthening of our faith. When we enter into God's Word, meditating on His writings, we are changed and molded through that Word and by His Spirit in a way that we could never accomplish through sheer determination. We are promised in His Word that our minds can be renewed (Romans 12:2) and that we have the very mind of Christ within us (I Corinthians 2:16). Just like the disciples our minds are "opened" by Him. We have the ability to truly understand the Word of God as never before. This is the kind of Bible study we were made to enjoy.

We Can't Get Away From It

In this kind of study, Jesus takes center stage. He is the center of history. He is the One who has changed everything for us, inside and out. He is the Father's greatest gift and the fulfillment of every divine plan. Without Him, none of the billions of people on earth have anything to look forward to besides a few measly moments of fleeting (weak) enjoyment that this life offers. He really is the center of all things good, the One to whom everything since the beginning of time has been pointing, and the only Source of life and peace. Is it not natural to conclude that since God gave us the book to explain His plan on a detailed level, it would be filled to overflowing with nothing but information about Jesus, who is *the* plan?

The really cool part is that God displays how incredible He is in the way He writes His Word. The Old Testament really is true history. It happened. Archeology continues to support the biblical account found throughout the Scriptures (although archeological data is always subject to interpretation). The Old Testament is the back story that leads up to the light of Jesus.

But it does not end there. The Scriptures are not just "back story." Throughout history, God has been telling the story of Jesus in every way. In nature, art, science, religion, and in the very lives of people—both individuals and communities—so that we are surrounded by it (assaulted by it?) and virtually drowning in it. In some way, God makes His plan known to everyone so that no one will be able to say they never "heard" of His desire or His plan to save them. When it comes to the Book He has, Himself, written to mankind, it is literally filled with page after page of the story about how He will accomplish the ultimate salvation offered to all people. This story is told through many different people, times and places, and each retelling brings to light some important yet slightly different aspect. As one backs up to see the bigger picture, all the tellings are clearly about the one and the same story of the great Savior's sacrifice for all mankind.

So let's say that because of the quotes from Luke 24 and just the sheer possibility that it *might* be true and what that could mean for your faith, you are willing to give me just a little more time to make an impact. You are likely ready to see something that will give some substance to this remarkably over-arching thought, if it actually does exist at all. Fair enough. Let's begin in a place that might seem a little childish at first—a place that virtually everyone has heard of, even if they have never been to church. Just don't be surprised if you find more in a lions' den than just a fanciful kids' story.

Chapter 2

Second Only to the King

Almost anyone you meet could tell you that the story of Daniel in the Lions' Den is a biblical story. But really, it is a story that is primarily reserved for the children's wing in churches across America. After all, it is very entertaining. There is a fantastic hero in the story who shows such excellent character traits as loyalty, courage, dedication to God, and complete devotion to his moral and religious principles, even in the face of certain death. The story includes a king, a righteous servant, vicious schemers, and maneating lions. There is conspiracy, intrigue, jealousy, deception, despair, anticipation, a twist ending—these are the elements of a real crowd-pleaser. Kids everywhere have heard it since their first year of Sunday school with gasps and smiles filling church classrooms (at least, when a half-way decent storyteller is there to make the presentation).

But the story almost seems a bit fanciful when one reaches adolescence, doesn't it? It's not that a Christian might think the story untrue (or, at least, we would not allow ourselves to admit it). After all, it is in the Bible. Yet we have allowed it to play such a major, almost exclusive role in children's curriculum for so long that it seems childish to spend adult study time on this enjoyable, seemingly lighthearted tale. Daniel is pictured in our minds in that same children's story book manner. He had an overnighter with a few large, playful cats and is now smiling and waiting for the next morning when he can wake up beside the previously ferocious felines (now also smiling) who have become his best friends. He will then exit amid astonished looks and pats on the back from a thankful crowd, including the king.

Of course, there is a grain of truth in this scenario. But, unfortunately, we have allowed the fanciful telling to take a foothold, almost becoming the actual story, itself. We have turned it completely into a wonderful children's lesson about God's protection (most certainly true) and, in the process, lost what the essence of this story points toward. Let us jump back into this story at the heart of the book of Daniel and take a closer look at what is really happening. Then we can get a better idea of why this story is so important to a Christian understanding of Scripture and to the foundation of the Christ story, itself.

In the Middle of the Book

First, notice the placement of this story in the book of Daniel. It is in the middle of the book. This is not a mistake, nor is it simply a coincidental location. Ancient Jewish authors (and authors of other cultures, as well) would place their most important pieces in the middle of their work. This is not a technique in modern western writing. We place our climax at the end of our written work. Everything written in our modern style builds and builds until the end where we place our most important piece—the piece that brings everything together; the piece that makes sense out of everything else. But in ancient

Jewish writing, that piece is generally found in the middle. The author was quite skilled and the story led somewhere even when read in simply a straight forward way from start to finish, like any other story. But the writer also used clues which could be detected by the careful reader. The clues led the reader to the literary center of his work where the most important point would then become clear.

Here we should clarify that we believe the Author of the bible, in its entirety, is the Holy Spirit. Men such as Daniel were moved by the Holy Spirit to write in a way that put God's points in the right places. Yet these authors often did not have a full understanding of their own writing (II Peter 1:20-21). Again, our biblical understanding is based on the fact that what Luke wrote in Luke 24:27, 44-47 is completely and totally true and that "all the Scriptures" are about Jesus. We recognize this means that no Old Testament author could have understood the full meaning of what he wrote. The authors were able to make connections to the circumstances they were experiencing in their time, but the full meaning—the one that pointed so clearly to Jesus as the coming, suffering Messiah—was hidden from them. But in hindsight, to his disciples, it became strikingly clear. The story of Jesus was everywhere.

Now back to Daniel 6. Consider the makeup of the book of Daniel as a whole. For the sake of brevity, let us speak in the most general terms. In the first five chapters, there are several major events taking place requiring Daniel's unique interpretive expertise. Nebuchadnezzar's dream in chapter 2, another dream in chapter 4, and a very mysterious event in chapter 5 involving the appearance of a hand writing cryptically on a wall during a large party—all find meaning in the God-given gift of Daniel. Only the former slave is able to offer understanding of such confusing and dumbfounding visions. Not only does Daniel interpret, but he seems to do so with ease, having a clear idea from the moment of hearing or seeing the mysterious portents. And he is always right.

But this is not so of chapters 7-12. Daniel 7 begins immediately with Daniel having his own mysterious dream. It is a very confusing dream, with strange beasts acting in strange ways, each one following on the heels of the last. But although Daniel has never had a problem interpreting someone else's dream, always receiving clear understanding immediately, his own vision troubles him and he is lacking clarity (7:15). Only when he approaches "one of those standing there" to ask for an explanation of what he has seen does he receive an interpretation of this disturbing vision (7:16).

Again, something very similar takes place in chapter 8 when Daniel sees a vision that leaves him "trying to understand" and requires interpretation from a heavenly being (8:15-17, 27). In chapter 9 another heavenly being comes to him to interpret a vision (9:23). In Daniel 10, Daniel receives another revelation that he cannot understand, and only after one is sent in response to Daniel's diligent prayer is interpretation given him through the heavenly messenger. Finally, Daniel is once more perplexed by what he hears and sees in Daniel 12, but is told by "a man clothed in linen" that the understanding is sealed up until the end (12:8-10).

So we have a strict division in the Old Testament book of Daniel. In the first half, Daniel can make clear and quick sense of the most puzzling visions. In the second half, Daniel is confused to the point of lying awake at night, frightened, needing the help of heavenly beings to make sense of disturbing scenes. The dividing line between these

Jesus in the Shadows

two halves is the story of Daniel in the lions' den. Since this story involves no odd visions or mysterious portents requiring divine interpretation, and because it falls in the middle of the book between two well structured halves, it must have another very important reason for its placement in this unique literary position.

Taking the Story Bit by Bit

For starters, please read the story in the Bible before going any further. As stated already, it is a fantastic story and one that will certainly hold your attention. It is only one chapter long, so you will be finished quickly. Then proceed to the following points that make up the story.

(Are you reading Daniel 6? You're not just saying you'll get to it later, are you?)

Now that you have completed the short but remarkable story at the heart of Daniel, consider the following:

1. There is a king over the known world. Darius is now the king of the most powerful nation in the world. He can do as he chooses and put anyone into any position he chooses. Ultimately, as far as the world is concerned, he has the final say in all matters. *There is no one above this king.* (Daniel 6:1-2; also see 6:25)
2. The king has decided to put Daniel in charge of all others who oversee his kingdom. Daniel's qualities as a leader are unmatched. The king is pleased with all that Daniel does and decides to make Daniel second only to him in all kingdom affairs. (Daniel 6:3)
3. All of the king's other administrators are jealous. These others have been in charge of the daily workings of the kingdom, but Daniel's skill and

integrity exceeds them all so the king decides to make everyone subject to Daniel's oversight. Consequently, the jealous leaders seek to find a reason to charge Daniel and remove him from authority over them. (Daniel 6:4)

4. Daniel is blameless. Because of his behavior and integrity, which is completely beyond reproach, Daniel's loyalty to the king and his devotion to the performance of his duties are completely faultless. The jealous leaders decide that only through a deceptive plot will they have any hope of ridding themselves of Daniel's oversight. (Daniel 6:4-7)

5. The king institutes a law that cannot be broken. The law says that anyone in the kingdom found praying to any god or anyone other than the king, himself, for thirty days after the law is put in place, must be executed. Of course, the king is talked into ratifying such a law by those who know that it will be the only way to trap Daniel into being found guilty of breaking one of the king's laws. (Daniel 6:7-9)

6. Only the death of the king's most beloved servant will suffice for the breaking of the king's law. Still, the king is inconsolable at the thought of his servant's death. Scripture states that the king "made every effort" to rescue Daniel, but was ultimately unsuccessful. (Daniel 6:11-15)

7. Daniel is found to have broken the king's law and is sentenced to death. (Daniel 6:16; the simple fact is that even though Daniel is made to look unfaithful to the king, he has never done anything that would in any way be detrimental to the king or the kingdom; see also 6:22.)

8. Daniel is put into a hole in the ground (what else is a lions' den, after all) and a stone is rolled over the hole, with the king's ring used to place a seal on the stone so that it will not be moved. With a hopeful yet seemingly futile wish for Daniel's safe emergence the following day, the king leaves Daniel to certain death. (Daniel 6:16-17)
9. The king is unable to sleep all night, refusing to eat or to accept any distraction that will take his mind off the fate suffered by his faithful servant. The next morning dawns to find the king at the mouth of the lions' den, calling past the stone that covers the cave to find out if it might even be possible that Daniel's death has, by some miracle, been overcome. (Daniel 6:18-20)
10. Although virtually unimaginable, Daniel is pulled from the pit of ravenous lions with "no wound found on him" (6:23). Daniel is completely whole. Not even a scratch is present to indicate that Daniel was in any kind of physical jeopardy.
11. Daniel's enemies are destroyed. The execution that was assumed to be Daniel's was instead suffered by those who plotted the death of the king's trusted servant. In other words, the way the evil plotters intended to destroy Daniel ironically became the way they, themselves, were destroyed. (Daniel 6:24)
12. Word goes out in writing to all nations and peoples that Daniel's God should be served by all. At the king's decree, all people on earth are strongly encouraged to honor Daniel's God as the living God whose kingdom is unending and who protects those who are His. (Daniel 6:25-27)

The term "lions' den" is really just a bit misleading for us. In actuality, what we have here is an execution chamber. In our day it would be a gas chamber, or a lethal injection room. It is not just a place where lions live—it is designed specifically as a place to have criminals killed. That is its purpose.

Putting the Jesus-Story Alongside

Now considering all that you've read in your Bible and our retracing of it above, place alongside it in your mind the story of Jesus we find in the New Testament. We will walk through it in the same manner as we have walked through the Daniel story, matching each of the twelve points above to a corresponding point in Jesus' life, ministry, death, and resurrection. (Point 1 below should be compared to point 1 above, point 2 to point 2, and so on.):

1. There is a Ruler over all the earth, in whom can be found all authority and power to accomplish His will on any level. This Ruler, of course, is God. All the nations and peoples of the earth are subject to Him. Nothing is outside His dominion (Deuteronomy 10:14; Psalm 24:1).
2. In the introduction of Jesus to the world, we find that God has placed all His authority and power in this One who will be considered only second to Him over all the earth (Matthew 28:18; John 6:40; 17:2). Jesus is blameless (Hebrews 4:15) and works only in line with the will of the Father in heaven (John 14:10).
3. Those who have been overseeing the affairs of God's people (from an earthly point of view)—namely, the Pharisees and Sadducees (the Jewish religious elite)—are very jealous. They despise the thought that this

Jesus in the Shadows

"latecomer" would be placed in charge of overseeing God's people, even above their own authority (Matthew 12:14; Mark 12:12). They looked for a reason to have Jesus killed (Mark 14:55) so that they might remove Him from their presence and reassert their own authority.

4. The search for a reason to have Jesus executed is unfruitful (Mark 14:55; Acts 13:28) because of Jesus' completely upright behavior (Hebrews 4:15) and superior handling of God's Word (Matthew 22:46). Consequently, the jealous leaders plot against Him in a subversive way to rid themselves of this One who has become a clear indicator of their own unrighteousness and out of control egos (Matthew 22:15).
5. God has set in place His Law, the breaking of which results in the death of the offender. Even though Jesus never broke the Law, Himself, the evil plot of the leaders resulted in the false accusation that Jesus cursed God, also known as blasphemy (Matthew 26:65).
6. Ironically, only the death of Jesus will account for the breaking of God's Law by sinful men (Isaiah 53:5; Romans 7:4; 8:3). Even though Jesus wishes for another way to make all things right between God and humankind, ultimately His death is the only means of reconciliation (Luke 22:42).
7. Jesus is wrongly sentenced to death as one who has blasphemed God's Law (Matthew 26:66). Jesus has never done anything apart from God the Father's will and does only what the Father wishes (John 5:19).
8. Jesus' body is placed in a tomb (a hole in the ground) with a stone rolled over the hole (Matthew 27:60) and

with a seal placed on the stone to ensure that no one tampers with the body inside (Matthew 27:66). There is no question that Jesus is dead (John 19:33-35).
9. King Darius called to his faithful servant in the morning, past the rock that covered the hole in the ground, hoping for a response. Likewise, God now breathes life into the body in the sealed tomb, raising it up on the third day (Hosea 6:2; Acts 2:24), eliciting the response that He desires.
10. Jesus appears to the disciples following the resurrection in bodily form, with the removal of all scars except those found on his hands, feet, and side (Luke 24:39; John 20:20). His body experienced no decay in the grave (Acts 2:27).
11. The ones who actually lost their place in the world the day Jesus was on the cross were the powers and principalities of the world (Colossians 2:15). The same cross that they sought to use to overpower their strongest adversary became the instrument of their own defeat.
12. Word goes out to all nations that Jesus' God—Jesus' Father—through Jesus, is the One whom all people should worship and to whom all people on earth owe total allegiance (Romans 16:26; Titus 2:11).

In this way, we can now see that the story of Daniel is not just an exciting story about Daniel. It is the central and key story in the entirety of the book, placed in the middle by the inspiration of the Holy Spirit for a most important reason. God is not simply telling a wonderful story about one of His faithful followers, willing to go to death, if necessary, for continuing to put his relationship with His God above all competing allegiances. If that were the end of the story (which we have often made it out to be) it would still be a very inspiring and powerful story of devotion and commitment to God. But it turns out that is only the tip of the iceberg. As a very close personal friend of mine (and a fantastic preacher of God's Word) has said: "We are not to be like Daniel because Daniel is a good, godly man; we are to be like Daniel because Daniel is like Jesus."

What's the Angle?

Each story of Christ's sacrifice in the Old Testament—each "type"—gives a slightly different perspective of the accomplishment of Jesus' mission. There are so many different aspects from which to view the central event in all of history, all having so many different ramifications. It takes the telling of the story from all sorts of angles to get a full perspective of everything that was actually taking place in Jesus. This would make sense as the disciples would have had only their "Old Testament" to use as a guide to understanding that what Jesus did on the cross was the plan of God from the beginning. There would be much that they could only discern over time, and they would have the Scriptures to use as their guide. As they studied the individual stories of the Christ-event, they would see it from different angles, each one giving a slightly different perspective on the event and its consequences.

In the Daniel story, one of the major emphases is that of blamelessness. It is emphasized near the beginning of the story when the other leaders seek to find anything of which they can accuse Daniel and again near the end of the story when Daniel's innocence is clearly displayed by God's protection (Daniel 6:4-5, 22). The king's faith in Daniel was never misplaced because no error was ever found in the loyal servant of the king.

The gospel emphasizes the sinlessness of Christ (II Corinthians 5:21; Hebrews 4:15). But thanks to Daniel, this utter blamelessness was foretold. Jesus was blameless, never doing anything that would in any way bring shame upon the King—His Father. In telling the story of the lions' den, Daniel has given us a glimpse of the Christ, undeniably righteous but falsely accused and sentenced to death, but then emerging from His tomb to once again take His place beside the King of the universe.

So, the real story is lying just below the surface. At the very heart of Daniel lies the Christ-story. It just so happens that what Christ tells the disciples in Luke 24 about the Messiah's rejection, death, resurrection, and the message delivered to all nations, is true. The most salient parts of the mission the Messiah will accomplish are recorded in detail in Scripture since the moment the first words were written. Not only did God know the plan, He inspired it to be penned over and again in the Book He wrote which would stand forever so that all men would know that there was never any other plan.

But what about that? Are there other places where the story is sitting just below the surface yet we've been too short-sighted to notice? Or maybe we were just never taught to see it. Oh, I'm certain we have no idea about many of them. But one of the places we do see is probably very familiar to many of us. It is in a story about the love of a father for a long-anticipated and celebrated son . . . a son whom that father has been told he will have to kill.

Chapter 3

Unswerving Trust

I'm not really a fan of the designation "Old Testament." Of course, it is much older, as a whole, than the writings of the New Testament. But, again, I feel the need to restate that what we refer to as the New Testament was not set during the lives of the apostles. When they needed firmly established writings which were widely accepted as having divine origin, they turned to the Old Testament. Because Jesus had opened their eyes to His **one** story throughout its multiple stories, it was the logical place to turn to make the case for Jesus as the Messiah who was foretold to be despised, rejected, killed, buried-for-three-days, resurrected, and ultimately proclaimed Savior of the world.

For the early Christians, it is likely that many of these stories became clear fairly quickly as they were already fluent with their Bible—that is, what we call the Old Testament. Jews grew up with a very strong emphasis upon the Law, the Prophets, and the Writings that Jesus mentions in Luke 24:44. The Scripture was the center of both religious and civil understanding. The schooling of children revolved around the religious writings. By the time the children were grown, there was a deeply rooted knowledge of the Word of God and how it applied to daily life.

What was not understood from the beginning, though, was how the Lord was making clear the plan that would come to fruition in the chosen Messiah. Although some aspects of the plan were known, many important details and the big picture were never discerned prior to Jesus' life, death, and resurrection (Col. 1:25-26; I Peter 1:10-12). For instance, when asked by Herod about the location of the Messiah's birth, the chief priests and teachers of the Law were quick to respond that Bethlehem was the birthplace foretold in the Scripture (Matthew 2:5-6). But the teachers and priests later proved they did not have a complete understanding of the Law regarding the Messiah's mission and person when they failed to acknowledge Jesus as the one sent by God to save all people. Even so, the Old Testament scriptures contain all the major emphases and events surrounding Jesus' life, death, and resurrection in order to fulfill God's plan of salvation. With eyes opened by our Lord, we are able to discern what was missed for over a millennium by those who thought their knowledge of the Law would save them.

A Strange Story of an Almost Impossible Command

Let's take a look at an example of what was missed by the experts but is actually a clear depiction of the plan God intended all along to carry out in Jesus: Genesis 22. Although this story is known to many Christians as being about Jesus' future sacrifice, there are several aspects of which many are likely unaware.

Take a little time now to read Genesis 22:1-19.

Jesus in the Shadows

What the careful reader must ask is, "Why were these particular events and details included in this way when God wrote His Word through Moses?"

Of course, there are several levels on which this question could be answered. One of those would be so the Israelites—the first hearers of the story—would understand the beginning and preservation of their nation. They would have a connection to the past. Abraham's continually deepening and growing walk of faith leading up to his willingness even to offer his only son to God if necessary is an excellent angle from which to view the story. But there is another very meaningful way from which the story of Abraham's sacrifice of his son (which he fully intended to carry out; 22:12) can be viewed as a whole—and it reaches far deeper into God's ultimate saving intentions in His own Son.

Now for a closer look at the story of Isaac's near-sacrifice. Consider the following:

1. The story is about a long-promised son, unlike any other, who has finally been miraculously born at a time after which many people would have long since given up waiting (Abraham was ninety-nine and Sarah was ninety when Isaac was born [Gen. 17:17, 24]).
2. Abraham is the one who prepared the wood on which Isaac would be sacrificed (Gen. 22:3).
3. There are three days between the time of Abraham being called to sacrifice Isaac and Isaac's near-sacrifice and figurative resurrection (Gen. 22:4; Hebrews 11:19).
4. Abraham seemed to know/believe from the beginning that both he and Isaac would return from the place of sacrifice (Gen. 22:5).

5. Isaac carries the wood on which he will be sacrificed to the place of his death (Gen. 22:6).
6. God, Himself, is said to be providing the sacrifice (Gen. 22:8).
7. Abraham is the one taking all steps leading up to the act of sacrifice (Gen. 22:9-10; it is strongly implied that Isaac is in full submission).
8. A strong male sheep—a ram—is provided by God in place of the human life that would otherwise be required (Gen. 22:13).
9. The ram is caught by its horns in a thicket when it is seen by Abraham (22:13). In other words, the sacrificial ram has thorns around his head.

Putting the Jesus-Story Alongside

I have no doubt that you've started making the connections all on your own already. It is astounding how many times we can read a story without seeing what it is really trying to say, isn't it? I think it is only prudent to take a bit of time here, though, to go over the same nine points of the story about Isaac's sacrifice, only with the Jesus story used to make the clear connection. After all, not everyone is as fluent with the Jesus story as some (let alone the Isaac story) and it is always good to hammer the planks into place firmly before continuing to build further out on the bridge. Let's do this with another nine points which line up easily with the nine laid out above like we did with the Daniel story in the last chapter (point 1 below matches up to point 1 above, point 2 to point 2, etc., just like before). Here we go:

1. The Jesus story is about a long-promised Messiah (Son of Abraham, as it were), awaited and hoped for, finally arriving by a miraculous

Jesus in the Shadows

birth at the proper time (Mark 1:15; Luke 2:25, 38; Hebrews 9:26)

2. God "prepared" the means by which His Son, Jesus, would die long beforehand, just as it was Abraham's job to prepare the means of death for his own beloved Son (Acts 2:23; Eph. 1:3-10).

3. Abraham's three days of anguish, knowing that he would take his beloved son's life by his own hand, correspond to the three days of Jesus' body lying in the tomb (Mark 8:31; 9:31; 10:34).

4. God knew that the final link in the chain was resurrection. Abraham's trust in God's unforeseen provision was recorded in a way that foretold God's plan from the very beginning to return in/with Christ (Acts 2:23-24; Ephesians 3:9; Hebrews 11:17-19).

5. Jesus carried the wood upon which he would be sacrificed (John 19:17).

6. Jesus is the "lamb of God" who will be a substitute for the life of all Abraham's descendants according to God's will (John 3:16; Galatians 1:4; 3:7; 4:4-5; I Thessalonians 5:9-10).

7. Jesus lived His entire life in complete submission to God's plan for Him (Luke 22:42; John 5:19; Hebrews 10:5).

8. Jesus is understood to be the "lamb of God" (John 1:29; I Corinthians 5:6; Revelation 5:7).

9. Jesus wears a crown of thorns upon the cross (Matthew 27:29; Thorns are introduced in Scripture as a punishment for sin [Genesis 3:18] and are, therefore, unbreakably linked with sin. It is no coincidence that it is thorns which keep the ram from escaping and that Jesus wore a crown of

thorns on the cross, symbolizing all of mankind's sin since the Fall which was placed on Him).

First Love

These events and circumstances which are included in the story of Isaac's sacrifice are certainly not merely coincidental with the events that took place on Calvary some two thousand years in the future. Although one or two similarities might be interesting, even eyebrow-raising, the nine above make a clear connection that has been seen by Christians throughout the centuries. But even with all of the similarities mentioned above there is still a particular note about the story in Genesis 22 that makes it one of the most wonderful allusions to the story of Jesus contained in the Old Testament.

The Hebrew word for "love" is not used anywhere in the Scriptures until this story. It is included in the chapter's second verse: "Then God said, 'Take your son, your only son, Isaac, whom you *love*, and go to the region of Moriah. Sacrifice him there as a burnt offering on one of the mountains I will tell you about." How wonderfully appropriate "love" would have no place in God's Word before it is used with such clear ties to the predicted death and resurrection of our Lord Jesus.

Surely it was with such clear details as these that men such as Paul, Peter, and the other apostles set out to win new believers to the Jesus movement. They did so by showing the irrefutable connections made with Scripture's most well-known stories. Such connections included the "three days," and the carrying of the wood by the one who was to be the offering, not to mention the thorns on the ram's head and the complete submission of the son, even to death. Connections like these would get attention.

Jesus in the Shadows

What's the Angle?

The near sacrifice of Isaac, as with all the "Christ-stories" found throughout the Old Testament, gives us its own unique perspective of the events surrounding Jesus' death on the cross. Perhaps the foremost of these is the submission of Jesus to the Father's will.

Even though Abraham will live to be one-hundred-seventy-five, he is definitely quite a bit older than middle aged at this point. Isaac makes a three-day journey with his father and carries the wood up the mountain on which the sacrifice will take place. Many Bible students throughout history have noted that Isaac would almost certainly be able to get away from his father, or possibly even overpower him if he felt threatened or if he was opposed to his father's wishes. Aside from the great surprise of God commanding Abraham to sacrifice this long-awaited, divinely-promised, miraculously-conceived son, the second most astounding development in the story has got to be Isaac's apparent willingness to become the sacrifice.

Isaac's trust in his father is positively unswerving. When he asks his father why they had everything to make a sacrificial offering except the sacrifice, itself, Abraham tells him that God will provide the lamb for the sacrifice (22:8). There is not one more word from Isaac throughout the story. As written, the point that comes across is that Isaac accepts the faith of his father as his own. He believes that his father must know exactly what he is doing and submits completely in trust.

As has already been pointed out above, this is the same kind of faith we see in Jesus. In Gethsemane, when Jesus is only hours away from crucifixion, He prays that God might allow for a plan other than the one to which He is about to submit. But He finishes that same prayer with the acknowledgement of, and complete submission to, His Father's plan which will require His sacrifice for the sin of the world (Matthew 26:39). Although He has all the power necessary to forcibly turn the tables on His accusers, He refuses (Matthew 26:53). Jesus willingly takes the role of the sacrificial lamb according to the Father's plan. In so doing, He becomes the ultimate model of submission to the Lord's will for all those who follow Him.

One Story Told Many Ways

Remember the Bereans from Acts 17? They were of "noble" character and "searched the scriptures daily" to find out if what Paul was saying to them about Jesus was true (Acts 17:11). These were the kinds of issues into which these noble people could look. But this is only the beginning. There are so many other powerful and intricately told stories in the Old Testament that are actually foretellings—in some amount of detail—of the story of Christ and His sacrifice. Each story comes with its own flavor. Each one is a view of the cross from a different direction. But all have the kind of connective tissue that, after some study, makes them unmistakable foreshadows of the center of God's eternal plan: the work of Christ on the cross.

That work is the single greatest event in history, and all of history revolves around the cross. For millennia before its occurrence, God was telling the Jews what He was going to do through them. After He accomplished that work, Jesus opened the minds of His disciples to understand the Scripture as never before. They could then see Him in the Law, the Prophets, and the Psalms, which was another way of saying the entirety of the Old Testament. It was all about Him. Finally, they could truly read their own book as it was ultimately intended to be read. Did that mean they would find Jesus behind every rock in the Scriptures?

Well, as a matter of fact, there is this one rock . . .

Chapter 4

Make Mine on the Rocks

Some people have their entire yards filled with rock. In some places, it's only practical. If the water needed to keep the yard looking nice is simply not available and the cost to make it available is prohibitive, then rock becomes a viable alternative. My brother had this very kind of yard when he lived in Albuquerque. The yard was already rock when they bought the home, but so was almost every yard in the neighborhood. It was simply not good money management and forethought to consider trying to keep a deep green landscape in that climate. (We are having a particularly bad drought in West Texas this year and if it lasts much longer we may all start considering the validity of the same stony approach.)

Jesus is a Rock

Rocky and dry go together in many places. One of those places is found in Exodus 17. It is a fantastic story about a wonderful rock found in a particularly dry place.

But before we go there, it seems only right to look at what Paul has to say about this very story in the New Testament. In I Corinthians 10:4, Paul states that the Rock from which all drank in the desert when the Israelites were

Jesus in the Shadows

with Moses was, in fact, Christ. Now this is a curious statement, to say the least. How are we supposed to take this? Is it one of those cute spiritual expressions, like when Jesus said He was the door (John 10:7, 9)? Jesus isn't a *real* door, after all. Neither is He a *real* rock. So He's kind of like that rock in the desert from which people got water to live, just like he is kind of like a door through which sheep can access greener pastures. So, in this way, it is just a cute turn of phrase.

It seems that Paul used the Old Testament (his *only* testament, remember) to create a nice tie-in for the story of Moses to the way our spiritual thirst is quenched by Christ. After all, Paul is going to need some ways to tie Jesus into the Old Testament. The Jesus-story needs some kind of foundation in the Torah if Paul is going to be able to preach Jesus' supremacy with any success.

But what if there is more to it? Perhaps Paul is simply making the very clear connection about Christ that is lying right before him in the text. Paul met Jesus on the road to Damascus, to be sure, and so learned by personal experience that Jesus was alive and well and that He is the promised Messiah. But Paul is a man of Torah. He knows that it will take more than his personal testimony to bring thinking Jews—and Greeks, for that matter—around to acknowledging Jesus' true identity.

Also, Paul is actually a Christian for well over a decade between his conversion in Acts 9 and going out on the open road in Acts 13 (see Galatians 2:1). What might he have been doing during this time? For one thing, he was arguing with Jews, *proving* that Jesus was the Christ (Acts 9:20-22). How else would he possibly prove anything to Jews about the Messiah except by using Scripture? So he was sharpening his skills. We only hear from Paul after he has been a Christian for a long time, having once been a disciple of the great Jewish teacher, Gamaliel, surpassing his peers (Acts 22:3; Gal. 1:14). All of his training and his detailed understanding and application of the law was, undoubtedly, helpful to him as he came to know the Jesus story intimately. God picked a man in Paul who would have an unsurpassed knowledge of the Old Testament. When he became aware of just how prominent the Jesus-story was throughout the Scriptures, he would make a formidable debater with excellent credentials as he argued for the obvious acceptance of Jesus as the long-foretold Messiah.

Above all things, Paul knows the importance of Scripture. He knows that it would do no good to play fast and loose with the application of God's Word if he expects to persuade any thinking Jew of the lordship of Jesus. Again, as a rule, Paul enters synagogues first when blazing new trails. He is extremely knowledgeable about Scripture, as would be most of his audiences, at least to some extent. This means that Paul must stay within acceptable bounds of interpretation if he expects to have a fair hearing and any kind of decent reception.

So back to I Corinthians 10:4—"For [the Israelites] drank from the spiritual Rock that followed them, and the Rock was Christ." We have no time to get into what Paul might have meant by "followed," but no matter what it was, he equates the Rock with Christ. Once again, how can he get by with this? In some way that works for his readers from Jewish backgrounds, Paul is making a link between Christ and the rock in the desert, which is central to the story in Exodus 17. Would someone so thoroughly versed in the Law and its correct interpretation make just a casual connection? Maybe . . . but it does seem unlikely.

Jesus in the Shadows

Painting with Broad Strokes

Of course, the best way to find out if there is more to this reference than a casual "cute" connection is to go to the story in the Old Testament. Take some time to read through Exodus 17:1-7 about three times slowly. Notice the details. Everything is important in some way.

(This is the part where you should be reading.)

Now, again, the rock is Christ, says Paul, and the people drank spiritual drink from that rock. Let's paint with broad strokes through this story—as we did in the previous two chapters—so that we can get a clearer picture of what is really going on.

1. There is grumbling among the Israelites (and many others since the multitude of people actually encompasses more than Israelites) due to a severe water shortage which they feel will eventually result in their deaths (17:1-3).
2. Moses asks why the people are quarrelsome with him about this and, in so doing, uses a parallel statement that equates their arguing with him to testing the Lord (17:2).
3. The people are almost ready to stone Moses out of their frustration with what they perceive to be his poor leadership (17:4).
4. God tells Moses what to do now that the situation has reached this fever pitch (17:5-6).
5. Moses is told to "go before" all the people with some of the elders (17:5). In other words, Moses is to get out in front of everyone so they can see him clearly and he is to make sure some of the leaders/elders recognized by the people are with him, also.

6. God orders Moses to take the "stick," or "staff" with which he struck the Nile with him in front of the people (17:5).
7. Moses must go to a rock at Sinai (the mountain where the covenant between God and His people was initiated; 17:6).
8. The rock must be struck with the same stick Moses used to strike the Nile. When that is done, water will pour from the rock to quench the people's thirst (17:6).
9. The place is named "quarrel" and "test" because the people were asking the question, "Is the Lord really with us?" (17:7)

A Bit More Detail

The story of the rock is a story of God's provision during desperate times, even for people who are belligerent and quick to forget past blessings. These people are being led by a man of God. Moses is a man unlike any other in Israel's history. He is sent to rescue the Israelites from slavery and to lead them through a long and difficult wilderness experience until they are finally brought to a new home—"a land flowing with milk and honey" (Exodus 3:8).

The passage starts with the people in peril. They are on a journey through a harsh, unknown land in which they are foreigners and strangers. It has become apparent that they will die in this land unless they receive help in a miraculous way. Moses—the one sent to them by God to save them from captivity and bring them to a new and wonderful land—is being confronted by the very people he came to save. They reach the point of being ready to murder Moses. It is at that point that God instructs Moses in the exact actions to take. Moses is to get in front of all the people, making sure that there are elders also up front. This will ensure that the elders have an excellent view of all God is doing through Moses. When Moses goes up in front of the people, he is to take with him a staff. The Hebrew word for "staff" could also be translated "stick" or "tree." But it cannot be just any staff. God makes very clear to Moses that the staff he takes must be the one with which he struck the Nile River in Egypt. We must ask at this point (if we are good students) why this specific staff is so important. The first plague in Egypt began with the use of this staff. As God commanded Moses because Pharaoh refused to listen to God and release His people, Moses took this staff and struck the Nile, causing it to turn to blood (Exodus 7:20). So, for the sake of brevity, Moses is to take with him the staff/stick/tree that makes blood flow when he goes before all the people and elders of Israel. He is then to take that same staff and use it to strike the rock. When the rock is struck, water will then flow from it and all the thirst of all those rescued from captivity is quenched.

After satisfying the people's need for water, the author tells us just how the place was named in Exodus 17:7. We read that the place where Israel received water was named "quarrel" and "test" because the people "quarreled" with Moses and "tested" the Lord. But this verse also gets very specific about just how the people "tested" the Lord by asking the question, "Is the Lord really among us?" This is the final line of the story. It is an important line. The people are questioning if God is truly present among them. The way the Lord chooses to answer is through the striking of a rock with a stick/staff/tree that causes blood to flow and for water to pour forth. The water will quench not just all of the former Israelite slaves' thirst, but also all of the foreigners who make up this great mixed multitude of people. In this way, the Lord shows that He is undoubtedly among them.

Putting the Jesus-Story Alongside

No doubt you are hearing how this story crosses over into the Jesus-story already. But let's get into some specifics that match up with the points listed above:

1. The people of Jesus' day are anxious for salvation (even though most of them likely see it in political terms—being "saved" from the Romans; Matt. 3:5-6). John the Baptist tells the multitudes that the time of judgment is upon them and they must submit to the Lord or perish (Luke 3:9).
2. The Jews argue with Jesus and in that same "conversation" Jesus equates Himself with the Father (John 10:22-30).
3. The leaders of Israel are ready to kill Jesus on several occasions because of their frustration with what they perceive is His lack of proper leadership/guidance. Most notably, the great crowd is yelling for his death on the day of His crucifixion (Matthew 26:4; Mark 3:6; 15:13; Luke 23:21; John 19:21).
4. God and Jesus communicate fully concerning His mission, with emphasis on the time of Jesus' imminent sacrifice (John 6:38; Luke 22:42).
5. Jesus' crucifixion took place before great crowds of people, Jewish leaders included (Matthew 27:39-43; Luke 23:48; Luke 24:18 shows Jesus' death is something widely known and discussed—one would almost have to be a foreigner to be unaware of it).
6. Jesus' carries His cross (which will be used to "strike" Him; John 19:17).

7. A new covenant is initiated by Jesus' sacrifice (Luke 22:20; Hebrews 8:8).
8. Jesus calls all who thirst to come to Him and drink (John 7:37). When Christ is figuratively struck by the cross, water and blood pour forth so that all people can have their thirst forever quenched (John 4:14; 6:35, 55; 19:34; throughout his gospel, John uses "water" in a way that leads to the cross, and he is the only gospel author to record that water also poured from Jesus after being pierced, along with blood).
9. The site of the crucifixion was a place where the people were asking a very similar question of whether God was really among them or not (though they certainly asked it sarcastically; Matthew 27:40-42). The irony is that God is with them in a way they could never have imagined.

So we see that the occurrence in the wilderness which took place at the rock so shortly after the Exodus event bears witness to much more than God's provision for the people's physical need. Actually, the Exodus event, itself, was a tremendous foreshadow of the Christ event. But, it will take many retellings of God's plan from various perspectives to get a clear picture of all that was taking place on the cross that incredible day. Paul made it clear that he sees Christ in this story as the Rock in the desert from which the people drank. The fact is that we are all thirsting to death without Christ. We cry out because we feel the same desperate need. And God, who is gracious, has sent Christ to be struck by a piece of wood that makes blood flow so that we can have our thirst quenched once for all. In that act He proves to us that He has not left us alone—He truly is among us.

What's the Angle?

The story of water from the Rock places a particular spotlight on the desperation of the people for the most basic of all needs to sustain life. The people reach a point of utter panic in their desire to have their thirst quenched. Although God has performed incredible miracles in their midst even recently, they are paralyzed by fear in their current circumstances. On the most fundamental level, death lies before them if they do not find water to drink. This need for water, and lack of trust in God to provide for that need, leads the people to the brink of murdering the one whom God has sent to be their savior—Moses. They fear that the mighty presence of God that was with them to save has somehow gone absent. Then they cry out for proof that He is still with them to provide miraculously, if necessary, whenever the need arises. Needless to say, they receive their proof.

In that display, however, is also encapsulated the story of all people, desperate for the healing, life-giving, miraculous work of God. We all go through life thirsty. We are all in need of the water that will sustain our spirits in the wilderness. That water is what only Christ can provide. When He was struck for our sins, His blood flowed out and cleansed us completely before God. Our thirst for righteousness ended. We now have access to the water that will never end and will never leave us thirsty again.

No More Hitting

Now, I would be leaving the story unfinished if I did not go further and make at least quick mention of the "rest of the story" found in Numbers 20:1-13. There are many similarities between this story and the one we just covered in Exodus. For instance:

(1) The people are without water
(2) The people gather against Moses (and Aaron) to express their desperation
(3) The people ask Moses why he brought them up from Egypt only to let them and their cattle die of thirst
(4) Moses goes before the Lord (along with Aaron)
(5) The Lord tells Moses exactly what he is to do
(6) Moses gets in front of Israel and also stands by the rock
(7) Moses strikes the rock and water pours forth for all Israel to drink
(8) The place is named "test" because the people struggled with the Lord in that place

As much as this story is similar to the one in Exodus—and it is *very* similar—there is a major difference. Although Moses used the rod in his hand to hit the rock, he was not supposed to. He was told very specifically in the story in Numbers to "speak to" the rock and the water would pour forth (Numbers 20:8). This is a major problem. So major, in fact, that it will keep Moses from being able to enter the promised land (Numbers 20:12).

As has been pointed out already, the stories are so similar that it is almost silly to think they are not supposed to be read together. One of the most basic techniques in ancient literature is parallelism. This is writing different parts of a story or work so similarly that it will become obvious to the engaged reader that the parts are meant to go together. The author is making a point which can only be understood by the thoughtful reader who discerns how the stories are interlinked.

Although many points could be understood by seeing these stories in connection to each other, the biggest point could never have been discerned before the work of Christ. Paul has told us already that the Rock is Christ. When we first see the rock, it is struck in order to keep the people from perishing. But the next time, with an almost identical story of people needing water to drink or else they will die, Moses is told very specifically to *speak* to the rock. That's right, just *ask* for water this time. There will be no more striking of the rock to produce water.

Like Paul said, the Rock is Christ. The New Testament makes clear that Christ died once for all for the sins of mankind (Romans 6:10; Hebrews 7:27). In fact, the writer of Hebrews strongly cautions his audience against taking too lightly the work of Christ which would be like crucifying (or striking) Him all over again, and such a path will lead only to destruction (Hebrews 6:4-8). In this way, Moses becomes the ultimate illustration. The "water" to quench all mankind's thirst was released from Christ when He was on the cross, struck for the sin of all people. There will never come a time when He will be struck again. Now, anyone who becomes aware of her deficiency of life-giving water from the Rock need only speak to the Rock to receive all she ever needs. It is very important that the Rock never be struck again.

In fact, to "strike" the Rock again (to crucify again the Lord of glory) will result, as it did for Moses in an earthly sense, in being restricted from entrance into the promised land (i.e., heaven). Of course, Moses was one of God's greatest servants. He is spoken of in only the highest of terms throughout Scripture and appears on the mountain in conversation with Elijah and Jesus regarding Jesus' own coming "exodus" (Luke 9:30-31). There is no reason to believe that Moses was excluded from the salvation that is enjoyed by all of God's servants in Jesus Christ.

But, what is being shown by excluding Moses from the earthly promised land is that for those who "strike" the Rock a second time (by not accepting the grace offered through Christ), there will be exclusion from enjoyment in the wonderful place to which God is leading us all—the heavenly "promised land." To cause the rock to be struck a second time, as Hebrews 6:4-6 states, is to draw close enough to Jesus to understand and even experience the gift of grace, but then reject it. For those who refuse to receive God's gift—who would strike the rock a second time rather than simply ask for the life that Christ gives—the entrance to God's salvation will be closed.

How the Disciples Understood Scripture

I have a very high regard for Scripture. As a Bible teacher and scholar, I have come to view Scripture with only the utmost respect. The rules that govern how one approaches Scripture are some of the most important principles, not just in my ministry, but in my life. I would never intentionally come before God's Word with an attitude of hearing only what I want to hear and simply seeing the meaning that I wanted to see before I opened the Bible in the first place (even though this certainly happens to all of us sometimes). Bible study is serious business. It is my greatest wish to understand the Scriptures properly and then to make correct applications so that they become thoroughly relevant to the lives of Christians today.

As I read my New Testament (such as the reference above from Paul in I Corinthians 10:4 and many, many others) I am compelled that the method of biblical interpretation for the disciples included the way of viewing and interpreting Scripture covered in this and previous chapters. This method of interpretation is known as typology. Actually, this way of discerning scriptural meaning is not new in the least. The ancient method of understanding Scripture used by the Jews included four different approaches to Scriptural meaning and one of those involved typology.

The renowned ancient scholar and church leader, Augustine, used typology in his understanding of Scripture. In writing of Old Testament events, he states, "These hidden meanings of inspired Scripture we track down as best we can, with varying degrees of success; and yet we all hold confidently to the firm belief that these historical events and the narrative of them have always some foreshadowing of the things to come, and are always to be interpreted with reference to Christ and his Church, which is the City of God."[3]

Church reformer Martin Luther believed very strongly in typological interpretation and used it extensively. At one point he states, "In the whole of Scripture there is nothing else but Christ, either in plain words or involved words."[4]

Some highly respected modern scholars are also aware of the obvious use of typology for scriptural interpretation. G. R. Osborne writes, "Throughout the New Testament one fact is clear: The entire Old Testament, not just the prophetic portions, is viewed as fulfilled in Jesus and the church he established."[5] In *Sacred Scripture*, scholar Richard Soulen agrees: "Indeed, the Scriptures employ typology so commonly, at so many levels, with such richness, sophistication and variety, that typology amounts to one of the key ways in which the Bible as a whole may be said to hang together."[6]

Jesus in the Shadows

Simply put, interpreting Scripture in this way is nothing new. There are guidelines that must be followed of course, and we can talk about those a bit more later. For now, let us only acknowledge that this approach to Scripture has a strong connection to the most ancient times. The people of those times were as intelligent as we are. They were just as in tune with the Spirit. They loved the Lord and adored His Word as much as we ever have. To think that their methods of interpretation were not sophisticated enough to discern truth (like ours) is to disrespect, in the most arrogant way, their love and devotion to God and their ability to understand His Word. (And this does not even touch on the fact that it would also mean that God did not answer their prayers to understand His Word properly like He has so graciously answered ours. Really?! How dare we?)

But let's return to Luke's words: " . . . [Jesus] interpreted to them in all the Scriptures the things concerning Himself" (Luke 24:27). *All the Scriptures* are about Him. Again, we could quibble about what "all the Scriptures" means, but the fact is Paul had no problem seeing Jesus as the Rock in the desert—a story where we would generally not go when looking for allusions to Jesus in the Old Testament. But the closer he got to the story, the more it made sense. For having wandered forty years in the desert, there just are not that many stories included about God's people during that time. It only makes sense that the ones God chose to include must be extremely meaningful for the overall accomplishment of His purposes and the ultimate purpose is, of course, to satisfy the desperate need of all people through the life-giving work of Jesus.

We can return to the first five books of Scripture (the books of Moses) a bit later. For now, let's jump to another story that is widely known among both those who love the Bible and those who are adamantly opposed to all it stands for, as well as everyone in between. It is the story of a young shepherd, a giant, and a very unexpected means of victory.

Chapter 5

Outmatched

Fights are never like the movies. I've seen just a few fights first hand in my time. But it was enough to make clear to me that no fight is ever going to be as well-choreographed as a Hollywood production. But I'm OK with that, because I've also seen just enough real-life fights to know that I don't care to see any more real-life fights ever again. I'm not saying there won't ever be a time where it's necessary. I'm just saying I'd rather not have to see (or, God forbid, be in) one. Ninety-nine percent of the time, fighting is ugly and messy and involves a lot of arm flailing and at least twice as many misses as hits. It is over quickly because the participants are almost always out of shape, and no one feels good in the end. Almost never is a real solution gained that can resolve the source of the argument. Simply put, it is generally just lack of forethought. Anyone who was trying to set up circumstances that would bring resolution to a rough situation would almost definitely pick a different way of doing it . . . almost.

So What is the Story Really About?

There is a story in the Old Testament with which we are all familiar. As a matter of fact, it is a story which has been passed down from generation to generation, even among non-believers, at least in its most legendary form. It is the story of David and Goliath. The most hardened atheist knows the basics of this biblical story. People who have never even read the story or heard the story in church can still give a rough synopsis. It is the story of a giant who, by all rights, is about to wipe the floor with a small though courageous would-be opponent. In the end, however, it is the smaller opponent that surprisingly and miraculously defeats his giant foe.

This is hardly a comprehensive picture of all that is taking place in the biblical story, though it does give a general sense of what is going on in I Samuel 17. But what is actually happening in the details that are included in the story is tremendously important. The story is about more than standing up for one's belief in God and His power to save against even the greatest threat (a real and worthy application, to be sure). The meaning that should get the most air time is the one that reaches to the heart of all God is doing throughout history.

(This would be a good time to read I Samuel 17. Go ahead. Return when you're done. I'll be right here.)

The story we've all heard so much about, and still hear almost constant reference to in all forms of popular culture, is certainly a great story. We view it as a story about underdogs, about how the least can defeat the greatest if he/she truly has the heart and will to do so. Again, there is something to be said for that application of the story, but only minimally. It is not the core of the story. In order to get a true understanding of the story we will have to view it

Jesus in the Shadows

through the eyes of those who understood what Jesus was all about when He came to earth, lived among us, and died for our sins.

We must try to view the story through the eyes of those who have no New Testament. Imagine that, like the apostles, the only Scriptures you had to understand Jesus and His work were the books of Genesis through Malachi—our Old Testament. In all of sacred Scripture, no other king of Israel or Judah had the desires of God so deeply buried in his heart as did King David. David is the most celebrated king of Israel by far and when the Messiah would return He was expected to be like David. It would come as no surprise, then, that the story of David would have a very strong connection to the story of Jesus. When the disciples and others looked into the Scriptures to find out if Jesus might actually be the Messiah (remember the Bereans—Acts 17: 11), this is one of the stories to which they would likely turn.

So let's look at it from that perspective, shall we? It is not just a story of the help God gives to those who trust in Him when they face overwhelming odds. It is the story that sets the entire tone for David's life. It tells us who he is and why God chose him to be the king of Israel. He best represents everyone who had God's will at the center of his or her life.

Not Getting Caught Too Quickly by Details

Now that we have read the story carefully, lets again tell the story by painting in broad strokes. They are not, however, so broad that they miss all details. But they are just general enough to allow for the story to be more than just a miraculous introduction story of Israel's second king. David's first self-initiated action is taken in this story. In that way, it sets the tone for his entire life. The kind of man/king David will be is illustrated in this first story of his heart and deeds. It is not just the first story told of David because it is the first thing David did. It is here because it is the story that gives the reader an overall view of the actions of a man who is "after God's heart"—a question the attentive reader has wanted answered since I Samuel 13:14. (The reader should read about this man after God's heart and say, "Wow, I wonder what that looks like.")

So here are the basics from I Samuel 17:
1. Israel is beset by the terrible and destructive forces of the Philistines, drawing up battle positions facing each other. The Philistines are led by a warrior so large and strong and with such venomous hatred that "Saul and all Israel" are "greatly afraid" at his presence as he boasts of his strength and ridicules God and His people. (17:1-11)
2. David--from Bethlehem--is the youngest brother and takes care of his very old father's sheep. His father, however, tells him to take provisions to his brothers and the other forces in battle against their enemies. He leaves the (safe) sheep in the hands of a keeper and then goes to the front lines of battle to provide for his brothers' needs (as well as others'), as his father told him. He arrives at the very time when the men of Israel are leaving to draw up battle lines. (17:12-20)
3. David delivers the supplies and meets with his brothers on the battle lines. He hears Goliath's taunts and sees the fear of the soldiers around him to take on the giant blasphemer because of his imposing size and obvious evil nature. Those around David say that the king is willing to give anyone who slays the evil

Jesus in the Shadows

Philistine three things--(1) riches; (2) his daughter's hand in marriage; and (3) to exempt the victor and his family from taxes or public service. David's eldest brother calls David's motives into question, accusing him of being only self-serving and wanting a good view of the battle, but not actually to get involved. (17:21-30)

4. David states to Saul that he will fight against this giant of God's enemies. Saul finds it very hard to believe that David would stand a chance. David assures Saul that he has defeated great beasts/enemies of sheep in the past and that he will certainly be delivered by God when he faces this intimidating and terrible foe. Saul allows David to go forward but wants him to at least dress the part. David is "not used to" (NIV) this armor, however, and goes to battle in attire and with weapons which would be deemed utterly inappropriate for the task at hand. (17:31-40)
5. Goliath does not see David as a threat. Goliath is angered by David's talk. He goes to battle with David in confidence that he will defeat him quickly and easily. David holds to his contention, however, that God will deliver Goliath into his hands. They meet each other in battle and David--very unexpectedly-- kills Goliath with only one shot from his sling and cuts off Goliath's head using Goliath's own sword. (17:41-51)
6. The men of Israel are emboldened by David's victory and pursue the forces that were arrayed against God's people now fleeing in fear. They pursue them even to the very gates of their cities. The battle is won--there is only a need to "mop up," if

you will. David's taking the head is an obvious symbol of his victory to all. He also took Goliath's armor—the spoils—for himself. But even at the end, Saul and those loyal to him have no clue as to who David is. (17:52-58)

The Really Short Version

It is a long story with several parts, but I have used six broad points to form a basic outline. The overall track of the story is telling much more than the story of Israel's second king, as was already stated.

Remember, this story sets the tone of David's life. The first decision we ever see David make is this one to stand as the Lord's servant in the face of even the most daunting odds. David is unflinching in his belief that God will use whatever means necessary to glorify His name in the face of such arrogance. David does believe that one of the two opponents is greatly outmatched in this battle. He just believes it is the tall one.

To tell the story in an even more concise way that gets to the heart of what is really being said: The father sends his youngest son with provisions to find out how the older brothers are doing as they battle the enemies of Israel. Upon arrival, the youngest son—though completely misunderstood by his eldest brother and accused of selfish motivation—takes matters into his own hands, refusing to allow anyone to speak arrogantly against the Lord or His people, no matter how imposing or terrifying that person may be. He eliminates Israel's greatest and most fearsome enemy in a completely unexpected and unforeseen way. The victory spurs Israel on to continue the battle by chasing the enemy, now defeated, back into the gates of their own cities. Even so, the leadership of Israel does not know who this young, brave savior of Israel is and are left scratching their heads even after the battle is over.

It is a beautiful story and it is one Christians know well because it is the story of the One and Only King of Glory, anointed but rejected, arriving in the midst of our battle against the enemy, eliminating our greatest and most terrifying oppressor in a completely unexpected way, giving us the courage and empowering us to rout the forces arrayed against us even though the leaders of those whom he came to save are clueless about his true identity.

Putting the Jesus-Story Alongside

Now that we've outlined the basics, let's zoom in on the specific ways this story of a shepherd boy defeating a giant is really just God telling us what's going to happen long before it ever did.

1. The people of God represent themselves, of course. The enemies arrayed against them and led by the most foreboding, evil, terrible warrior imaginable are none other than the spiritual forces of the evil one arrayed against God's people (Ephesians 6:12) and led by Satan, himself, spewing taunts and slurs about both God and His people. Remember, Satan is both a killer and a liar (John 8:44).
2. David means "beloved" and comes from the Hebrew "love." That's right—the root of David's name means "love." Jesse comes from the root "to be" or "to exist." So, in essence, the "existing one" sent His Son, "love," into the world to provide for His people in the midst of spiritual battle. He brings "food" from His Father (Matthew 4:4; John 4:32-34; 6:51). Like David, Christ left the sheep that are safe in good

hands in order that he might seek and save those who are lost (Matthew 15:24; Luke 15:4; 19:10). Like David, Jesus is from Bethlehem and his Father is very, very . . . very . . . old. Jesus arrives to help God's people—his brothers (Hebrews 2:11)—in the midst of the battle. He, Himself, is the food sent by the Father (John 6:51).

3. Jesus came to do as his Father wished and delivered to the people all that was sent, fully carrying out the Father's will (John 17:4). He is incensed by the taunts and arrogance of the leading enemy of God's people—Satan (Matthew 4:10). It is the sons and daughters of God—the Church—that are Christ's bride (Ephesians 5:23-32; Revelation 21:9-27), whose hand He will receive in the greatest of weddings at the end of time (Ephesians 5:27). He also can assure all his brothers that they (we) will be given all the riches of glory in Him and will be sons of God (John 1:12; Ephesians 2:6-7; in other words, exempt from taxes in God's Kingdom as would be any child of the King, Galatians 4:7).

   Just like David, Jesus has an "older brother" that is not pleased with Him at all. Like many older brothers in Scripture, Jesus' older brother, Israel, seeks to harm or even kill Him, primarily motivated by jealousy of the F/father's love (see Cain and Abel, Ishmael and Isaac, Esau and Jacob, Judah and Joseph). Eliab accuses David unjustly as Jesus is accused unjustly by the Jewish religious leaders (Mark 15:3).

4. Jesus came claiming that He was here to do battle with the strong man, to bind him, and plunder his house (i.e., get God's people back; Matthew 12:29). It

is very difficult for most of the religious leaders and the majority of Israelites to accept that He could be successful (remember, the people said things like, "Isn't this the carpenter's son?" Matthew 13:55). They saw Jesus and were unimpressed. Many did not see a king who could lead into battle, which is what the people of Jesus' day believed they would need if they were ever to defeat their oppressors (John 6:15). But Jesus tries to assure the clueless disciples that He is able, by God's help, to overcome even death at the hand of the enemy (Luke 9:22). Still, the people would rather Jesus act/dress/present Himself differently. But He refuses to act the way they would have him and goes to the greatest battle--that of the cross--with what would be considered weak armor and weaponry, indeed. Just as Saul and Israel's soldiers must have thought, the people of Jesus' day must have been thinking, "this can't possibly end well" (Luke 24:21).

5. Satan knew Jesus was his enemy, of course, but believed that He could be defeated. Jesus is angered by Satan's temptations. But successfully withstanding them, He commands Satan out of His presence. Jesus never loses confidence that God will defeat Satan through Him. Jesus never swerves from the Father's will. Just as David, Jesus runs to the battle (Revelation 19:11). Through the cross, Jesus defeats Satan completely and certainly unexpectedly (I Corinthians 2:8-9). David cuts off Goliath's head as Jesus crushes Satan's (Gen. 3:15). David uses Goliath's own sword to cut off his head just as Jesus uses the very instrument that Satan would have used

to kill Him to utterly defeat Satan (Colossians 2:13-15).

6. Ever since the cross, our battle is won. We are the ones who assault the gates of Hell which will surely not stand against us (Matthew 16:18). Jesus is the victor and he has taken the spoils of victory. But still, even after the defeat of Satan by the cross, Israel's leaders remained clueless as to His real identity (Acts 4:18; 5:40).

Again, I have only here given a view of this great passage which includes the more obvious features. There are many points which would go to establishing the fact that this cherished story is intended by God to be a foretelling of Jesus' work on our behalf, but this should suffice to show the basics and to make the case in a broad sense.

Remember, also, that this is the first story of David's life following his anointing. He has just been made king and his first kingly decision is to completely and utterly eliminate the lying, blaspheming enemies of God. Surely there were many stories of David's young life which could have been included first. But this one is chosen for a reason. That reason is because it establishes the tenor of David's whole life as a Christ story. It is a summary of all that Christ will be about in His kingship.

A Big Step Back

You don't have to be a photographer to see what a wide-angle lens can do. Before cameras were on every phone and apps were used to make cameras do everything short of wash dishes, only cameras took pictures. Back then, you needed special lenses to take different kinds of pictures. The difference between a photo of the Grand Canyon taken with a regular lens and one taken using a wide-angle lens was striking. The scope that was captured with a wide-angle lens was unmistakably greater and showed so much more of the grandeur than any standard lens could.

It is very often this way when we are seeing the Christ-story in Scripture. We need to see things with a wide-angle point of view. We need to step back from the story far enough to see what is going on from a distance. When we close in on it too much, we become so caught up in the details that we fail to see everything and thus lose sight of the big picture. In this and previous chapters, I've referred to this kind of seeing things from a wide-angle point of view as "painting with broad strokes." It is the same principle. We are trying to explain the stories in the Old Testament in general enough terms to see how they may fit into the Christ story. Since Jesus, Himself, tells us that the Old Testament is all about Him (Luke 24:27; John 5:39), we are obligated to use the tools and techniques we have to see just how pervasive His story really is.

In this story we have simply stepped back enough to see that, when painted with broad strokes, the story of David and Goliath is really the story of a Son sent by a Father to join His brothers in their desperate battle against evil, completely destroying the most evil and terrifying warrior in a way that no one would have guessed possible, even though the leader(s) of the people—those who *should* have been directing and leading the battle—were completely ignorant of this hero's identity and origin.

This does not mean that the details do not fit or are unimportant to telling the Christ story, also. As a matter of fact, all the details are extremely significant. Consider the meanings of the names of David and Jesse. Also, the fact that Goliath is almost completely arrayed in bronze although David refuses to wear Saul's helmet which just "happens" to be made of bronze is a fantastic and wonderful piece of symbolism in itself (I Samuel 17:5-6, 38). Yet it would not serve our purpose to chase this particular rabbit trail here. For now, it is enough to know that although Goliath is virtually covered in bronze and Saul tries to give David his own bronze helmet, David refuses such battle gear, setting him apart from any kind of earthly or demonic battle expectations.

The wide-angle view helps us see the story in its basic format. If it seems to fit the Christ-story in some way, we can close in little by little on the details to help us make sense of just how each detail fits.

Knowing When God's Talking

It is the Holy Spirit's purpose to teach us about Jesus (John 15:26). This promise was made to the disciples when they had nothing but the Old Testament. They needed to be taught about the Jesus story throughout the Scriptures. Then they could take that incredible teaching with them as they traveled throughout the empire (and beyond) showing how the story of Jesus was foretold since ancient times. They could also show how it was the one story that really held everything else together. Meditation—sitting before God's Word and allowing Him to show you His insights in His time—is essential to the process of learning from the Holy Spirit.

Ultimately, it is our goal to know God through Jesus Christ. We may see many things throughout our day or hear many voices from different friends, colleagues and even strangers and ask, "Was God trying to show me something there," or "Was the Lord speaking to me through that person?" But we can answer a wholehearted "yes" when we pose these questions of Scripture. We can always trust that

God is speaking to us when we are in His Word. How wonderful to know that He is anxious to lead us to great and life-changing insights. He has gone out of His way to lay a book in our very hands filled with nothing but words directly from Him.

Even so, hearing is not doing, is it? There have been many in the past who have heard the words of God and not changed a thing to come in line with His instruction. Some of them have even heard Him speak His words to them directly. One such man in Scripture found himself on the wrong end of a deep sea fishing expedition because he refused to do the will of God which had been clearly spoken to him. But even he could not side-step God's overriding will to tell the story of Jesus through Him.

Let's go fishing . . .

Chapter 6

Because I Said So

    Obviously, I realize the response, "Because I said so," is not a great form of motivation for many children. Even so, it worked for me and my brother.

    We had a terrific father. I cannot imagine loving any father more. Even though he was taken from this world by a deadly disease when I was only twenty-two, the lessons I learned from him continue to be useful in my life on a daily basis. But when my brother and I were particularly young, my father was a single parent, my mother having been killed in a car accident when we were only fifteen months old. (Yes, we are twins.) Being a single parent is stressful in the best of times so from the age of fifteen months through eight years, dad was the one making all the decisions for our family. I'm sure frustration reared its head often in the early days of that time. My brother and I were taught to be well-behaved, however, and we were generally not difficult children to have around . . . so I'm told. But we could still be kids, of course.

    I remember more than once during a trying time of expressing our "kid-ness," the easiest and quickest way for Dad to get us to do what he wanted without having to really answer the "why" question was with the response, "Because

Jesus in the Shadows

I said so." That was a way of saying any number of things—"I don't have time to explain," or "We are not in a good place to get into it," or "It's something that you will like if you will just give it a chance," and many other translations. But the tone was one that said, "This is my last statement in this conversation. Either do it, or we'll move on to consequences." So, as you can imagine, "Because I said so" was usually all that was needed to elicit my brother's and my cooperative response.

Apparently, Jonah did not learn this lesson in the same way. Jonah doesn't ever ask why but the general results are the same. God told Jonah to go to Nineveh and preach and that should be enough (Jonah 1:2). That should be all that is necessary to get the job done. But it's not. Jonah does not wish to go. He hates the idea so much that he books passage on a ship that is going in almost the exact opposite direction from where he is told to go (Jonah 1:3).

But before we get into the story of Jonah any more, let's look at how Jesus used Jonah's experience to allude to his own fast-approaching fulfillment of God's plan.

In Matthew 12, Jesus finds Himself in another confrontation with Pharisees. Remember, the Pharisees are the religious elite of Jesus' day and to say they know the Scriptures well would be a *huge* understatement. In Matthew 12:38, they ask for a sign from Jesus, as if He hasn't given them enough already. Jesus, of course, knows that their hearts will not be won over by a miraculous sign from Him (many of them just saw Jesus heal a man with a withered hand in 12:13). Rather than even attempting to appease them, Jesus points out that they represent an evil generation. He states that no sign will be given to them except that of Jonah the prophet (Matt. 12:39-40). He then equates his own future experience with that of Jonah's in the past, stating that he—the Son of Man—will have a very similar experience to Jonah. Just as Jonah was in a fish's belly for three days and nights, so will Jesus be in the heart of the earth. Of course, Jesus is likening his experience following His death to what Jonah experienced when he attempted to run away from doing God's will and taking the message of judgment to Israel's enemies.

The Pharisees, like Jonah, were not friends of non-Jews. They took the Law very seriously and those who were not a part of the Jewish bloodline—true descendants of Abraham—would never be on a level playing field with those who were. Keeping this in mind, it seems interesting that Jesus would choose this particular biblical reference to give to the Pharisees. They don't want to accept Jesus. Actually, they are in direct opposition to Jesus and to believing that God is working in Him. They refuse to accept that God's will is to follow Christ. Like Jonah, they do not wish to go along with God's plan. Isn't it appropriate, then, that Jesus would quote this particular Scripture to them. By referencing Jonah, Jesus draws attention to a very well-known story of one who was in very close contact with God but who did not like how God was going about His plan getting out His message. But like it or not, the Pharisees are told the only sign they will get is the sign of Jonah. End of discussion.

Again, this is your wonderful opportunity to go to the Scriptures and begin by reading our passage for yourself. This should be easy since there are ten fewer verses in the entire book of Jonah than were in the single chapter telling the David and Goliath story which we just covered. I'll take a break from talking so much and you just come let me know when you are ready. As usual, I'm not going anywhere.

Jesus in the Shadows

Now let's get back to Jonah and just cut right to the chase: Jonah is a Christ-figure. One of the interesting—though not unique—parts of the Jonah story when considered from this perspective is how reluctant Jonah is, throughout the entire book, to be a participant in God's plan. Even by the end of the book, Jonah is still completely unhappy with the outcome. But he has reluctantly accepted that there is no other choice but to go along with God's will. God has made clear to Jonah that He will accomplish His purpose through Jonah whether he is a willing participant or not.

But let us step back from the story and see what is being said in a big-picture sense by painting, yet again, with some very broad strokes:

1. God calls Jonah to make His judgment known to an evil, Gentile nation (Jonah 1:2).
2. Jonah refuses to accept God's call to preach judgment to Gentiles and, instead, travels—among Gentiles, ironically—in the opposite direction from where God has told him to go (1:3).
3. God sends a terrible storm against the ship which threatens to cause the death of everyone on board, yet even though Jonah knows the cause of the storm and how to avoid it, he sleeps below deck while certain death looms over all (1:4-5).
4. Even after being awakened by the Gentiles who only want to find favor with God and be saved from their deaths, Jonah wants no part of their eventual turning to God and chooses to die instead of simply getting on board with God's plan. He puts himself into the hands of Gentiles telling them that the only way for them to have

peace with God is to kill him. Although they show their desire to save Jonah's life by trying to get back to land first, they finally admit there is no other hope to escape death and accept Jonah's direction. Still, they pray that God will forgive them for killing what they believe to be an "innocent" man because it seems clearly to be God's will that they do so (1:6-14).

5. The Gentiles throw Jonah into the sea, supposedly causing his death. They are then saved as the sea becomes calm and God's wrath is appeased. Jonah is swallowed by a great fish, being kept "safe" by God inside the fish for exactly three days and three nights (1:15-17).

6. Jonah prays to God from the belly of the fish, figuratively referencing having been "barred in" by land and God "raising up" his life from the "pit." After three days, God has the fish vomit Jonah out onto dry land (2:1-10).

7. Again, Jonah is told to take God's message of judgment to the evil, Gentile nation. Now being assured there is no way out of God's will for the message to come from him, Jonah reluctantly goes to the great Gentile capital of Nineveh and proclaims God's coming judgment (3:1-4).

8. The Gentiles accept Jonah's message and repent in all sincerity resulting in God's forgiveness (3:5-10).

9. Jonah expresses his great dislike with the outcome of God's plan. The very reason he did not wish to be part of the plan from the beginning was because he foresaw that the likely result would be the forgiveness of the Gentile enemies

of Israel. Even at the end of the book there is only God's attempt to reason with Jonah regarding his hard heart and Jonah's silence on the subject of whether he will ever accept that God's plan was right (4:1-11).

Actually, it could certainly be argued that the strokes with which I have painted this time are not really so broad. As I said before, there are fifty-eight verses in I Samuel 17 (the David and Goliath story) and a total of only forty-eight verses in the entire book of Jonah. Our synopsis might not be that far from the length of the book, itself. But still, it is helpful to tell the story in more general terms just to get a big-picture idea of how the action is flowing without being so focused on specific names of people, places, and so forth. This allows us to see "through" the story to larger and more encompassing principles that God may be trying to put across.

In fact, simply to stay consistent with previous chapters, here is the story of Jonah in an even smaller nutshell: God calls an Israelite to preach of coming judgment to Gentiles. The Israelite refuses. But God will not have His plan foiled by the Israelite's refusal. God uses the Israelite's attempt to escape his duty as the way to save Gentiles. The Israelite's (supposed) death was his own idea which he suggested in the first place so that he could avoid being part of what he thought was a bad plan all along. After three days and nights, and an undeniably miraculous rescue, the Israelite very reluctantly must accept that God is going to accomplish His purpose through him with or without his full cooperation. Even after the preaching is done, the Gentiles have repented, and God's forgiveness has been extended resulting in the salvation of many thousands of previously condemned Gentiles, the Israelite is unhappy with the outcome of God's plan and the reader is left to wonder if the Israelite will ever accept willingly his part in God's plan to share forgiveness with these Gentiles.

There you go. That is the end of the story. A strange ending, to put it mildly. The reader is left dangling. Will Jonah ever come to accept God's will for preaching to and then forgiving the Gentiles through him? We do not know.

Jonah Without the Fish

That's right—the Jesus story is kind of like the Jonah story without the fish. The Jonah story is no longer just a big fish story, you might say (overused pun alert!). Now it can be seen for what it really is: another incredible retelling of the one and only story that actually fills the pages of the Old Testament. It is told from its own perspective, of course. It has its own principles and angle to emphasize, which we can get more into shortly. But it is the same story, that much is certain.

Now I am sure you can see where we are headed at this point since we have been through this process several times. But still, I would hate to stop using a good pattern when it has been so helpful up until now. So let's go through our points again, this time with Jesus in mind, and show just how closely related a mythical sounding fish-story is to the story of the One who calls followers to be fishers of men.

1. The Israelites were always called to make God's existence and will known to the Gentiles (Exodus 12:48; Numbers 15:15; Isaiah 56:6-7).
2. Israel continued to hate the people groups around them, always looking down on them and seeing them as undeserving in regard to God's promises (Luke 10:30-36; Acts 13:46-50; like

Jesus in the Shadows

Jonah, as Israel increased in its discrimination of Gentiles, it found itself more and more at the mercy of those same Gentiles, being surrounded by them and having their collective fate in the Gentiles' hands [aside from God's divine protection, of course]).

3. The storm that threatens to kill all at once is, simply put, God's judgment which rests upon all people. There can be no doubt that all were going to perish together—Jew and Gentile, alike—without the gift of life through Jesus Christ (Romans 3:23). The sleeping Jonah represents the fact that even though all are about to perish together in a raging storm, Israel's lack of concern is blatantly obvious as seen in Jonah's ability to sleep until awakened forcefully by the ship's captain.

4. Israel's leaders continue to refuse to follow the plan of God, especially as made clear through Jesus. Rather than try to see the possibility of God's plan in Jesus, the leaders hand Jesus over to be killed. All of Israel (all who would be saved) are caught up in Jesus on the cross (Romans 6:6). So just as Jonah represented Israel and gave himself up for death, the religious leaders hand over Jesus who also represents all who will be saved in Him. Just like Jonah did not wish to be a part of saving Gentiles which he considered unworthy of God's grace, so, too, were Israel's leaders completely unwilling to accept the message of inclusion preached by Jesus. In both cases, it was assumed that by handing over the one in question to die,

participation in God's plan (or what Jesus *said* was God's plan, in the case of the religious leaders) could be avoided. But in both cases it was the death (near death of Jonah) which was actually the heart of God's plan all along.

    Also important to note is the reluctance of the Gentiles to take Jesus' life, just as the Gentiles in the story of Jonah tried to find another way. In both stories the Gentiles declare the "innocence" of the one they are putting to death (Matthew 27:24).

5. The Gentiles put Jesus to death and God's wrath is appeased (Mark 10:33-34; Isaiah 53:5). Jesus' body is then kept safe in the earth, undergoing no decay (Acts 2:31).

6. Jesus references the three days which Jonah spent inside the fish as being similar to the three days He will spend in the tomb (Matthew 12:40). Jesus is laid in a tomb (a pit, a hole in the ground; figuratively "barred in" by the earth) following his death (Matthew 27:60) and after three days is "raised" from the pit (I Corinthians 15:4).

7. Whether Israel likes it or not (and many do not), the message of salvation has gone out from them (Acts 1:8; 13:44-47). From Israel, the word of salvation has gone out to the Gentiles. Just as God used Jonah's hard-hearted action to bring the message of judgment and then subsequent salvation to the Gentiles in a very unorthodox manner (three days and nights in the belly of a fish), so God used reluctant and belligerent Israel, in all of their fighting against His desire to forgive (even putting the Savior to death), to become the

source of the message of salvation for all Gentiles (Romans 11:11).
8. The Gentiles, though dead in their sins, received the word of God's judgment upon their sins in Christ, repented of their sins and received the gift of salvation (Ephesians 2:1-7).
9. From the time the New Testament is completed and even until now, there is no full resolution regarding Israel's collective dislike for the inclusion of Gentiles in a plan of salvation which they believed was specifically for them (Acts 13:46-50; Romans 10:19; 11:11; however, many believe that Paul is referencing the ultimate turning of the Jews as a whole to Jesus at the end of the age in Romans 11, a chapter which is clearly about this very subject).

Truth or Fiction

Many scholars have questioned whether or not Jonah could possibly be a true story. Quite frankly, I believe that it is. I also believe that Job is true, that Jesus did all the miracles in the gospels as described and that the Red Sea really did part right down the middle to allow the Israelites to cross. If this makes me a fundamentalist, then I must simply plead guilty and be settled with it. But, after all is said and done, there is a level on which whether or not someone believes every word of Jonah is literally true becomes somewhat less important. This is the level of the Jesus-story.

I don't know if you know anything about the Dead Sea Scrolls, but here is one really fantastic point that can be made. The Dead Sea Scrolls can all be dated to have been written between about 150 B.C. and 50 A.D. They contain full copies and/or pieces of every book of our Old

Testament (aside from Esther), and some other books, too. This means that every book of our Old Testament had to be a well-established, well-circulated part of Jewish religious experience at least by 50 B.C., and very likely a good time before 150 B.C. That includes Jonah, of course. Now if the Jonah story is really just the story of God's salvation for the entire world through Jesus, even with Israel's reluctant participation, and if the Jesus story is told in such wonderful detail as I believe it is, and it was a well-established part of Jewish Scripture at least a hundred-fifty years before Jesus (likely much longer), then what is being seen in Jonah is really God's plan whether the story actually happened as told or whether it was inspired fiction that was made a part of the Holy Scripture by God to be another unmistakable way of telling the story.

    As if there wasn't enough evidence from Jewish history already, the Dead Sea Scrolls are physical proof that the Jonah story could not have been tampered with after Jesus (as if that was even possible). The story of Israel's history and of God's plan of salvation for all the world was told long before Jesus became a baby in Mary's womb. If this is just another way of putting the Jesus story at center stage in the Scriptures, then it is worth our full attention even if we choose to think it is nothing but a fable (which I will state again that I do not).

    Simply put, God is telling the Jesus story in detail long before it ever happened. He is telling it so precisely that it cannot be missed—at least by those who are not bound by jealousy or personal agenda. Remember that Jesus, Himself, found it strange that the disciples were having such difficulty with the suffering and death of the Messiah since it was foretold so clearly in Scripture (Luke 24:25). Whether one believes a man was kept alive inside the belly of a fish for three days or not, the fact is that the Jesus story is being told *long* before it occurred, and that is what should make us take notice.

One Man Represents a Nation

In the Jonah story, one of the major points which comes across is how one man represents the entire nation of the Jews. All of Israel is caught up in Jonah. But really it is no surprise that God would choose to tell His story this way. After all, the story of Jesus is the story of all people who love God and seek His grace being caught up in His Son. In Jonah is found the story of Israel with all her jealousy and anger toward her enemies and her pride about the fact that she is special before God. After all, they alone were chosen and rescued by Him and given His own written Word as no other nation in history. This pride became a wall that kept them from seeing others outside their nation as being worthy(?) of God's grace as they believed they were. But reluctant though they were, God used them to carry out His mission to forgive all peoples of the earth who would come to Him. Even those who put Jesus to death would later find themselves caught up in that death and become a part of the mission to all people.

As an aside, Jonah is certainly not the only person in Scripture whose story is told from the viewpoint of representing an entire people group. The Elijah story, the Sarah story, the Samson story—even parts of the David and Moses stories-- are all told from this perspective. It is quite common. Simply because we are not used to reading this way does not mean that others have not been so trained. Paul, himself, uses Adam, Abraham, Sarah, and Hagar as representatives of massively large people groups because of the way the Bible relates their stories as individuals. Our fierce individualism has often led to an inability to see clearly what is best for the whole. The Israelites (and many other cultures) have always been a people who placed needs of extended community over needs of the individual. They have no problem seeing themselves as part of a collective. I would strongly contend that this is a mindset to which the church should return, as well—not to mention that it will give us a much better mind for understanding Scripture, which is the point of this book, after all.

What's the Angle?

The story of Jonah is no different from any other Christ story in the way that it is telling the story of God's Messiah from its own unique perspective. We do get something from Jonah that is especially important about the Christ story that won't be found just anywhere. You can probably figure out quickly what I believe this perspective to be but I will include it anyway simply for the sake of being complete, if nothing else.

Jonah tells us the Christ story from the perspective of the reluctant Jews. It is a view that predicts how Israel as a whole will respond to the idea of a Messiah that is the hope of the entire world and not of the Jews, alone. At the same time, it is the story of how God will use that reaction as an integral part of His plan to save all people and how Israel will then sulkingly sit off to the side, unwilling (for how long, who knows) to accept that God's grace was, through them, extended to and received by even the worst of sinners and their most hardened enemies.

Grace for our enemies is not an easy gift for anyone to extend. I do not here condemn the Jews for their actions any more than we should all be condemned for our selfish hearts. They were taken right where they were and used by

God to fulfill His greatest plan. The story of Jonah allows us to see just what an incredible God we serve who can extend eternal, all-powerful love even through those who are far from understanding their role in God's plan to give salvation to all.

And on the subject of not understanding one's role in the salvation process, there is a great story that comes to mind. It's about some older brothers who got very jealous with a certain younger brother whom they thought dad liked a little too much . . .

Chapter 7

Stuck in a Well

Most of us have heard about Lassie informing less attentive humans of difficult and even life-threatening situations which can only be remedied by species with opposable thumbs. Many people now jokingly make reference to these wonderful episodes of canine heroism by saying at some point in a lighthearted conversation, "What is it, Lassie? Is Timmy stuck in a well?" This is generally followed by laughs from those who may have seen or heard of the old episodes. Of course, the laughing is not because someone is stuck in a well but because of the idea of being able to understand a dog as she communicates the whereabouts of her young, trapped owner. Lassie would be helpful to Joseph in Genesis 37.

The last major life story of an individual in Genesis to be covered in detail is about Joseph. Joseph was the son of Jacob and it was Jacob that was renamed "Israel" by God. This is because Jacob was the father of the nation of Israel in a very real sense. Jacob had twelve sons which, in turn, became the patriarchs of the twelve tribes of Israel.

Jacob had two wives: Leah and Rachel. They were sisters. Between these two sisters and each of their handmaids (one handmaid apiece), Jacob had a total of at least thirteen children (twelve boys and one girl). Of course, it is not a part of this book to get into the ancient practice of having children through the handmaids of one's spouse, and frankly, I'm glad it isn't. What is important for our current discussion is that Jacob never made any pretense about the fact that the favorite of his two wives was the second one—Rachel. Also, the sons borne by her were his favorite children. Only two of the children were born to Rachel, and it took a very long time and a miracle of God for Rachel's womb to be opened. The firstborn of the two was Joseph. This made Joseph the most special of all the children in Jacob's eyes (Gen. 37:3). Jacob never had any qualms about showing this favoritism, either. In the story of Genesis 37, it is shown primarily in the gift of a very special, multicolored coat.

But just like the future tribes of Israel, the sons of Jacob did not always get along. In fact, at the beginning of Joseph's story, things are about to turn very bad in what can be assumed is basically an eleven-against-one situation. (Not all brothers show the same amount of hatred for Joseph as others and this will be discussed in more depth shortly.)

Brotherly Conspiracy

Walking through Genesis 37 slowly and painting with a broad brush will give the reader a better view of the basic themes that are making up the chapter. In the same way as previous chapters, let us walk through this chapter of Genesis and give some general points that show the story's makeup from a wide perspective.

But first, as usual, please take the time to read Genesis 37. It's a grand total of thirty-six verses, so it will not take long. Read slowly and try to take in the details.

Then come right back here and we'll walk through this chapter in a few big steps.

(And you're reading, right . . . ?)

It's a very interesting chapter, isn't it? Talk about a dysfunctional group of brothers. The last straw seems to be a new suit of clothes given to a sibling who is already disliked for sharing dreams that make him look superior. A murder plot is then touched off which morphs into a slave clearance sale. But let's not get ahead of ourselves. Here are the basic points that make up the chapter:

1. Joseph is one son of many. He is the most-loved son of his "very old" father—a fact well known to all Joseph's brothers. Consequently, he is despised by them. Joseph tends flocks with his many brothers and has brought back at least one bad report to his father about his brothers' poor shepherding habits. (37:1-4)
2. Joseph has dreams which seem to indicate a time when all of his brothers, and even his mother and father, will serve him. His brothers are angered by the dreams and their interpretation, and his father seems skeptical, at best. But the father makes sure to keep the dreams in mind. (37:5-11)
3. The father sends Joseph away from home to check on the welfare of his brothers and the flocks they are shepherding and then to report back. Joseph's first discovery is that his brothers are not pasturing the flocks where the father expects them to be and he must go to a different location to find them. (37:12-17)
4. When his brothers see Joseph approaching, they first plot to kill him, although one brother—the eldest—is reluctant. They strip him of his precious robe—the

father's gift to him—and throw him into a dry well (in other words, an empty hole in the ground) to leave for dead. (37:18-24)
5. One of the brothers (Judah) comes up with a plan to make money by selling their hated brother to Gentiles as a slave and the other brothers are convinced by him that the plan is a good one. (37:25-28)
6. The older brother who did not wish to be party to the murder plot later returns to find the pit empty and the younger brother gone, at which time he is completely dismayed about what to do next. (37:29-30)
7. A goat is slaughtered and the blood used to cover the precious robe that belonged to Joseph. The brothers then use the robe to trick the father into believing that Joseph has been killed by a wild animal. Even though much time goes by and all of Jacob's children try to provide comfort to him, he utterly refuses their attempts and states that he will mourn until the day he dies. (37:31-35)

There is much more to the story of Joseph in the final chapters of Genesis. In fact, the Joseph story will continue right up until the end of Genesis and Joseph's name will then be mentioned in Exodus 1, making a smooth transition to the next book of the Bible. The fact is that the Joseph story, as a whole, tells the story of Jesus in very detailed fashion. There is no doubt that Joseph is a Christ-figure, by the end of the story being empowered with all the authority over the known world, second only to the supreme ruler—Pharaoh. The details fit marvelously and are varied and incredible but are not part of the scope of this chapter. Here, we simply wish to give a small taste of how the Jesus story is told through the initial chapter of this story about Jacob's second-to-last-born son.

What we can see, however, is that even in this first chapter about Joseph, the story is being told in a way that gives the reader a clue into the incredible work that God will do through His great Son in the future. Of course, it won't be understood until much later, when the disciples can look back on the Scriptures and see exactly what Jesus meant when He said that everything which happened to Him was told in God's Word long before His earthly ministry.

Small Jump

In the Joseph story, the distance between the original story of Jacob's favorite son and the story of God's beloved Son is really not that far. Where bigger leaps may need to be taken in the stories of David and Goliath or Jonah, for instance, in the story of the most-liked son that the father sends to check on his brothers, who then grab, strip, and sell him to Gentiles, the leap is greatly minimized.

Staying true to form, let us work through the current story according to the points we have established above, showing how Jesus' own ministry and passion are paralleled in Genesis 37:

1. Jesus is God's beloved Son (Matt. 3:17; 17:5) as no one else ever could be or will be. His Father, God, is known as the Ancient of Days (Dan. 7:9). Although He was born a Jew and came to His own people (His brothers), He was despised by them and the world hated Him because He testified about its evil deeds (John 7:7).
2. Many prophecies/visions in the Old Testament indicate obedience and service to the Messiah by the

Jesus in the Shadows

Jews, as well as all nations (Deuteronomy 18:15-19; Isaiah 11). The Jewish leadership (and Jews as a whole) refused to accept Jesus as their king (John 19:19-22; Acts 2:36). At one point, however, Jesus' mother Mary—although seeming frustrated with Jesus' assertion as a young boy about his place and doing His Father's business—treasures the event in her heart (Luke 2:51).

3. Jesus is sent by God to be among His people (John 1:11; 3:16; 5:23). Jesus finds the people to be like "sheep without a shepherd" (Mark 6:34) and their leaders are more like hired hands than shepherds (John 10:12). In other words, they are not shepherding as they were instructed by the Father just as Joseph's brothers were not tending the flocks in the place where the father expects.

4. As Joseph's brothers did, the leaders of the Jews devise a plan to kill the Father's most loved Son (Mark 3:6). But not all the Jewish leaders wish to see Jesus dead. Some very high ranking Jews are clearly on Jesus' side (Luke 23:50; John 7:50; 19:38-39). Jesus is stripped of his precious robe by those who kill him (Matt. 27:28; John 19:23-24). Jesus is then placed in a tomb (a hole in the ground) with death being clearly established (Mark 15:45; Luke 23:53; John 19:33).

5. Jesus is essentially sold by one of those closest to him who guarantees to hand Him over for a price (Matt. 26:15-16). Like Joseph, Jesus is eventually turned over to Gentiles by his relatives (Matt. 27:2).

6. Jesus' followers, upon returning to the tomb, are greatly dismayed to find the tomb empty and, like Joseph's brother, are confused about what they might possibly do next (John 20:1-2, 15).

7. The blood of a goat is significant since this is the animal used once a year, every year, on the Day of Atonement as a sacrifice for the sins of all the people (Leviticus 16:15). Jesus is the "lamb of God that takes away the sin of the world," of course (John 1:29). But goats are particularly associated with sin (compare Matt. 25:31-46) which, in this case, is what is being highlighted. Joseph's brothers then use the coat to trick Jacob into believing that Joseph was killed by a wild animal. Jacob is utterly grief-stricken and his refusal to be consoled, even after "many days," is meant as a display of God's heart—in human terms, of course—regarding the loss of His precious Son. (Although we do not have a record of God's "grief" stated as such in regard to the crucifixion, the typological clues are numerous as we have already seen once in our closer look at the king's reaction to Daniel's sentencing in chapter 2.)

Joseph is Different

Joseph is a different kind of Old Testament character than almost anyone else. With such a detailed story being told about him, one would think that we might hear something about his faults as well as his positive character traits. But this is not the case. Even though a very large part of the first book of God's Word is taken up by his story, Joseph is never once portrayed as having one unlikable or sinful character trait or behavior. Although some have seen in Joseph's telling of his visions to his family a kind of superiority coming through in Joseph's assumed tone, this does not have to be the case at all. The visions should simply be read as Joseph telling his brothers and father what he saw. It would not have to be his superiority that caused the jealousy and derision of his brothers. It seems more likely that the brothers are ready to feel badly toward Joseph at the slightest provocation because of their father's obvious preference for him. Even though this dislike may be understandable on some level, it is not justified by Joseph's words or actions.

We say Joseph is different from *almost* any other Old Testament character because of another character we have already covered—Daniel. Daniel is also spoken of in glowing terms in almost every case. Of course, their stories are remarkably similar as well. Consider the following:

a. Both receive obvious preference from primary authority figures in their lives (father first and later Pharaoh for Joseph; the king for Daniel).
b. Both are jealously despised by those with whom they had close connection in daily duties (brothers for Joseph; satraps for Daniel).
c. Both are given the gift of dream interpretation by God.
d. Both interpret the dreams of the most powerful ruler in the known world.
e. Both are set up by those around them to be convicted of breaking the law (Joseph by Potiphar's wife; Daniel by the satraps).
f. Both are thrown into a hole in the ground by those who jealously hate them.
g. Both are raised up to the position of second most powerful person in the known world, having all the authority of the greatest king on earth given to them.

This is a simple comparison to be sure. Digging deeper will yield even more fruit connecting the two stories to one another. Both are, of course, simply Christ stories.

God used the lives of two different men who lived more than a millennium apart to tell the same story of His love for His Son and the way His Son would be thrown into a hole in the ground at the hands of jealous men who refused to receive the authority given to Him by the all powerful Ruler of the world. Also, in both figures, righteousness and blamelessness are key attributes showing the close correlation to the Jesus story by alluding to the perfection of Jesus.

Out of Order

In the way the story occurs in Genesis 37, there is a particular point that is out of place. You may have noticed when reading through the outline that the selling of Joseph into the hands of Gentiles occurs after Joseph is thrown into the hole in the ground. This should not be used to discredit the story's relationship to the Christ story in any way.

Never will every detail of a typological Christ story fall exactly into place to make a perfect foretelling of the story of Jesus. To expect this would be to ask too much of the original story. First of all, the typological Christ stories are told through sinful, human vessels. Even though very little, if any, is said in a way that alludes to Joseph's or Daniel's sinfulness, many others are written of whose lives are marked with the sinful choices they make and yet who are used by God to tell the Christ story according to His divine organization of events. We just saw this in the Jonah story in the last chapter. The same can actually be said of Moses, David, Jacob, Samson, and many others. These are only types—shadows, the writer of Hebrews would say—of the reality. They cannot live up to the reality but can only give a glimpse, in a small way, of all that the reality actually is.

Secondly, in this case it is clear that the basic points of the story of Jesus are all present in the first chapter of the Joseph story. These include (1) the foretelling of all of Israel's tribes being subject to the One most loved by the Father; (2) those same tribes being jealous of their "younger brother;" (3) the plot to murder the most-loved Son; (4) selling the Son; (5) handing the Son over to Gentiles; (6) throwing the Son into a hole in the ground; and (7) the empty hole in the ground discovered later by one of the brothers (now greatly distraught) who did not wish to see Joseph killed but was reluctant to stand up against the others. Although there is a slight deviation from the way the Christ story is told in the New Testament, because of the sheer number of very strong similarities in such a short space it seems easy to conclude that the story of Jesus is related here long before it actually occurred.

Finally, in this particular case, the selling of Joseph and his being handed over to Gentiles falls in the perfect place. Because this chapter shows him thrown into the well/hole first, then sold, then his brother returning to save him, we are set up for Jesus' burial, followed by the discovery of the empty hole by a distraught brother. It becomes the way in which the Author (the Holy Spirit) accomplishes His goal of telling the aspect of the Christ story which involved the dismay of Jesus' followers when they discovered the empty tomb. So two goals are accomplished: (1) making the point of Jesus being betrayed and handed over to Gentiles, as well as (2) the discipleslater confusion and distress at finding Jesus' body missing. In essence, it is just great storytelling.

What's the Angle?

Before we get away from our discussion of this story which concludes the first book of Scripture, as in other chapters let's take a quick look at the particular angle this story gives us on the life of Jesus. Although there are various emphases, as always, and each one could be mentioned and explored to have a greater understanding of what is actually going on in the life of the Messiah, one thing that comes to the fore early in the story is the great love the father has for his precious, late-born son. Jacob has waited many years for his (most-loved) wife to finally have a child. The son that she has quickly becomes his most-loved son of all. Jacob does not try to disguise the love he has for his son and even does what he can to show it off by giving a wonderful and unique gift to this special boy and by giving him the job of making sure the older boys are doing as they are supposed to while tending the sheep.

Of course, it is easy to argue, from an earthly point of view, that Jacob has terrible parenting skills. Any novice family counselor will tell you that showing such clear favoritism for a particular child among many will only result in a terrible outcome in the long run. But this is not the story's point. As stated before, God uses those whom He has chosen to tell the greatest story of all time, even with all of their faults, failures, and terrible choices. Ultimately, Jacob's awful paternal example is not what matters. The key to the story is found in the fact that God used Jacob's awful example to showcase His own love for His most precious Son. By not being an impartial father, Jacob creates a situation within his earthly family that is very similar to what is found between God and the earthly "sons" He created. Just as Jonah's sinful actions were used by God to tell the story of all He would do to save a world through Christ, so

Jesus in the Shadows

Jacob's imbalanced display of love for his sons allowed for a telling of the Jesus story in a way that would spotlight God's unmatchable love for His Son, Jesus. God has no problem showing His unrivaled love for His Son in a way that is obvious to all, and whether His people like it or not is their problem, not His.

The Joseph story is a fantastic telling of God's provision for His people during times of trial. He establishes a savior from among His own people—a savior they reject and who is then accepted by Gentiles as the second most revered leader in the world, and who then ultimately saves his own family. In both macro- and microcosm, this is the Jesus story. Joseph has become another one of the incredibly numerous ways that God has told the story of His ultimate plan of redemption from the beginning.

Jesus in Hi-Def

The story of Jacob's most-loved Son certainly tells the story of Jesus in a clear and distinct way that leaves little doubt about its ultimate aim. But I believe that in some places, it gets even clearer than this. One of these places is with a man whom we would expect to be seen as the great forerunner of our one and only Savior, Jesus Christ. The universally-acknowledged, greatest savior of God's people prior to Jesus was none other than Moses. Without a doubt, Israel looked to him as God's chosen leader to rescue His people from bondage and lead them to a place that would be their new home—a land filled with milk and honey—where they could live under God's care and provision for all their days. If there is a leader in Scripture that is the clearest type of Jesus—the story of salvation in hi-def before the story ever took place—it is told in the life of Moses. There is a story in Moses' life that quite possibly tells the Jesus' story better than any other in Scripture. Let's go see Jesus on the big screen.

Chapter 8
Pinhole Camera

When I was in fourth grade, a solar eclipse occurred which could be seen where we lived in Big Spring, Texas. Of course, we were instructed not to look at the sun during the eclipse. This is because the harm caused to eyesight (of an unprotected eye) is still as great during an eclipse as it is in direct sunlight. Actually, my fourth grade teacher was adamant enough about this rule that she shut the students up in our classroom and turned on the television so that we could watch the eclipse with the chance of harm to any student's vision being completely eliminated.

But there were other classrooms that were allowed to make what are called pinhole cameras. This homemade craft allows one to view a small "reflection" or facsimile of the solar eclipse as the sunlight passes through a pinhole on one end of a box and creates an image that can be viewed on the other end. In this way, one is outside in the sunlight (or darkness, during the eclipse) experiencing the eclipse to a certain degree, yet never looking directly at the eclipse which could easily result in at least partial blindness for the rest of one's life. Nothing to fool around with, for certain.

Moses will soon find himself in a similar situation as we read the section of Scripture highlighted in this chapter. But it won't be blindness Moses could risk by looking the wrong direction. It will be death.

Again With the Middle

When reading through Exodus, some would say that things get a little "slow" after Chapter 20. Chapter 20 is the giving of the Ten Commandments—a passage at least heard of by almost everyone. Immediately following the Ten begins a section having to do with applying the Law to exact situations. Following this, in Exodus 24, Moses is told by God to come up on the mountain with Joshua and receive the Law from God directly. For forty days Moses will be on the mountain with God in God's very presence, where no man had ever stood (except Adam, before the first sin).

Chapter 25 begins a full description of laws and specifications about the tabernacle, precisely how it is constructed along with its various furnishings, the clothing the priests must wear, how to make the priests ready for service, and the importance of Sabbath, among other instructions. These directives, on the one hand, and then their completion, on the other, actually become a mirror image of one another as we go from chapter 25-40.

Without going into detail, however, it will simply be pointed out that this way of organizing ancient writing is the same style (only more elaborate) as was discussed in chapter 2. There, we discussed how the story of Daniel in the Lions' Den is "pointed to" by the way the whole book is organized. The ancient author would write in such a way that his most important point would be stressed by placement in the center. (Of course, the reader must take the time to put the pieces together to discover it). In this book, our point is not to get into the details of how well-constructed this entire section is. What we will do is go to the center of this section—the part found right in the middle of all the various instructions about the tabernacle and all its furniture. This is where the rubber meets the road—or, for us, where the Old Testament collides with the gospel full force.

Mountain Climbing

The people have not been freed from slavery in Egypt for very long by the time we reach Exodus 32. But it has been long enough to get a giant group of people to move in the same direction, leave Egypt, cross the Red Sea, travel through some wilderness for many days, get into a fight, and start organizing a reasonable system of dealing with issues that arise from having so many people displaced together.

Now the people are at Mount Sinai. The Israelites have been here long enough to hear Moses tell them the Ten Commandments and the laws associated with them and they have willingly committed to doing everything that the Lord has said (Exod. 24:3). At this point Moses goes up the mountain where he first eats before God with Joshua, Aaron, Aaron's sons, and seventy of Israel's elders. But then Moses is called up to meet with God personally in the cloud that descended on the top of Sinai. Moses takes Joshua with him and enters the cloud—into God's incredible, powerful presence—where He stays for forty days and forty nights (Exod. 24:18).

From the beginning of chapter 25 through the end of 31, we read the many instructions having to do with the building of the tabernacle, all of its furniture, the ordination of priests, the clothing they are to wear, the importance of

Sabbath observance, and more. But when we reach the beginning of Exodus 32, the story of what is happening between the people and Moses and God starts up again.

This is where you should begin reading—at Exodus 32:1. Read through 34:35. Yes, I do understand that it is not "normal" to read three chapters in one sitting for most Christians. But this is one story and needs to be understood that way.

(Maybe it would be good to turn to Nehemiah 8 to see the people gathering in the square and standing for the reading of the Law from "early morning until midday" [Neh. 8:3]. Just imagine—standing outside, from early morning until midday, listening to someone read Genesis through Deuteronomy simply because you are so glad to be in the homeland that your grandparents told you about and to get to hear the Law of God that sets you apart from all other nations in the world. See? Kind of makes reading three chapters in a row sound pretty easy. Actually, make it six and go ahead and read it twice. It is going to be so good to have it stuck in your head when we start getting deep into this. Trust me.

And, reading now . . .)

While the Cat's Away . . .

Well, now that you have read the passage, you can easily see that the people have not had their selfishness decreased to any noticeable extent. Even though Moses has always been there for them and they have made it through some faith-stretching experiences up to this point, they are still quick to think the worst. Moses has been gone for forty days now and the people have lost all patience and no longer expect his return, even though he told the elders he

Jesus in the Shadows

and Joshua would return to them after they spent time with God on the mountain (Exod. 24:14).

Let's walk through these chapters and take our usual wide-angle view to get an idea, in general terms, of just exactly what is going on here:

1. The people grow skeptical of Moses' return because of his long absence. Aaron gives in to the people's demand for a god/idol to worship and the people follow their sinful desires (32:1-6).
2. God instructs Moses to leave His presence and go down to the people. God is considering destroying the people so that He might start over with Moses. Moses intercedes on the people's behalf and God changes His mind (32:7-14).
3. Moses descends the mountain with God's Law, sees the people in their sinfulness and shatters the stone tablets. Moses asks Aaron why he brought such great sin on the people. Aaron responds by blaming the people for their great tendency to sin and claims ignorance about how the false god was made (32:15-24).
4. Moses calls the most faithful men of Israel to himself to destroy many of the unfaithful (about 3000) and to call others to the Lord (32:25-29).
5. Moses tells the people he will "see if I can do something to keep this sin from being held against you" (CEV) and asks God to blot out his name with theirs. God responds that He punishes those who deserve it and that the people can go to the promise land but that He will not go with them (32:30-33:6).
6. *The Tent of Meeting (33:7-11). (This is a special piece of our puzzle that we will return to later.)*

7. Moses argues for the Lord to go with the people into the land and the Lord agrees based upon His relationship with Moses (33:12-17).
8. Moses requests to see God but God tells Moses that no one can see Him and live. God places Moses in a hole in a rock from which Moses will get a glimpse of God. (An allusion to death followed by being placed in a hole in a rock.) The Lord passes by giving a description of Himself and restating specific laws which Moses writes on stone tablets that he carved out of rock and brought with him (33:18-34:28).
9. After being in the hole in the rock and after writing the Law, himself, at God's direction for forty more days, Moses returns to the people. The people are frightened by Moses' transformed, glowing appearance so Moses approaches them with a veil on but takes it off when going into God's presence. Moses encourages the people to follow all the laws given by God (34:29-35).

Waiting for Someone Different—but the Same

There is the short version. It is quite a story and has quite an interesting placement in Scripture. There are few places more sacred to the ancient Jews than Sinai. Moses was a figure unmatched in the Old Testament for his intimacy with God and for his complete devotion to God's lead. Even with Moses' later disobedience in Numbers 20 (which we considered at the end of chapter 4), there was still no one who could come close to Moses' position before God in the mind of the ancient Israelite. After all, in this text we have just read that "the Lord used to speak to Moses face to face, just as a man speaks to his friend" (33:11). No one else in the Old Testament gets such

Jesus in the Shadows

incredible words spoken of their relationship and communication with God. Truly, Moses was different.

But, even with all of this, the Jews understood that Moses was not intended to be completely unique. In Deuteronomy, the Jews are about to enter the promise land. But the man who has now led them for forty years through the trials of the wilderness will not be the one to lead them into this great land "flowing with milk and honey." They are unsure how they will accomplish all they need to without the leadership of Moses. But in the final speech of Moses before entering the land, Moses tells them God has promised they will not be without such a leader.

In Deuteronomy 18:18, God says through Moses, "I will raise up a prophet from among their countrymen like you, and I will put My words in his mouth, and he shall speak to them all that I command him." In the original context of Deuteronomy, this man turns out to be Joshua—the prophet like Moses who will lead the people into the land God is giving them. But even though Joshua was an excellent leader and led the people with God's will always foremost in his mind, the ancient Jewish people continued, throughout their history, to expect another.

We are sure of this because of a few passages in John that make very clear the people's expectation of a great prophet who was set apart from all others in history, except perhaps for Moses, himself. Four times in John the people use the phrase "the Prophet" in a way that shows there is one special person they are waiting on whom they believe will lead them as only Moses ever has. The people are not waiting for just any prophet or "a prophet," but "*the* Prophet."

In John 1:21 and 1:25, John the Baptist is in a conversation about his own identity in which there is a question about whether or not he might be "the Prophet" which is to come. John, of course, denies that he is "the Prophet." Again, immediately following the miracle of feeding five thousand people with only a few loaves and fish the people begin to say that Jesus is surely "the Prophet" who is expected to come into the world (John 6:14). Finally, after His teaching about Himself to many at the Feast of Tabernacles, some of those who have heard Jesus begin to say, "This really is *the Prophet*" (John 7:40; emphasis mine).

Just as we said, there are many who have been waiting for someone "like" Moses (Deuteronomy 18:18). Even though Joshua was a great leader, they still await someone who will be a leader in a way that Moses was and that Joshua never completely fulfilled.

Like Moses

As we have already mentioned, in Exodus 32-34, Moses is clearly depicted as a leader like no other. On the mountain, he is in God's presence in a way that no one has ever been. He is inside the cloud with God and is described as talking with God as a man talks to a friend. Even David does not have such glowing words spoken about his relationship with God.

But, of course, we believe Jesus is *the Prophet* who was like Moses in the most perfect way—the way no one would have predicted but the way that fits better than anyone else in history. Let's take a closer look at this story of Moses compared with the Jesus story and see just how the One "like Moses" is tied to the story of the ancient Israelite deliverer.

1. By Jesus' day, many people have given up on the leadership of Moses—which means they have given up on trying to understand or follow the Law of

Jesus in the Shadows

Moses. Many now go their own way and do what they wish with their lives, ignoring Moses' leadership and God's instruction in His Word (John 8:39-47). Like Aaron, the religious leaders of Jesus' day have set up for the people a false god, made up of tradition rather than God's true Word about Himself (Matthew 15:6; 23:23).

2. God sent His Son from His presence to His people (John 3:16; 6:29; 7:16; 8:42). If not for Jesus all people would be destroyed (Ephesians 2:1-7). Jesus intercedes with God on our behalf so that we are not destroyed (Romans 8:34).
3. The coming of Jesus among His people signals a time of the replacement of the covenant written on stone with that written on hearts (Jeremiah 31:31-34; see number "8" below). Jesus confronts the religious leaders with their poor leadership and bad example (Matthew 23:1-7, 13, 15; Mark 3:4-5). The religious leaders of Jesus' day do not accept Jesus' evaluation of their leadership (Mark 3:7; Luke 20:19).
4. Jesus calls faithful followers to Himself who, on the first day of the Holy Spirit's filling of believers, will baptize about 3000 followers of Christ (Matthew 4:18-22; 9:9; Acts 2:41).
5. Jesus gave himself as a sacrifice to take away the sin of all people (Romans 5:6, 17-19; II Corinthians 5:14; Hebrews 10:10). Without Christ, we have no hope of God being with us on our own journey through this world, i.e., our wilderness (Ephesians 2:12).
6. *The Tent of Meeting (33:7-11). See below.*
7. Based upon God's love for Christ and upon Jesus' sacrifice for us, God, through Christ, is now with us

at all times on our "journey to our promise land" (Matthew 28:20; John 14:17; Romans 8:9).
8. In order that all can be made right by God's plan, Jesus dies and is placed in a tomb (a hole in the ground; Luke 23:46, 55; Acts 2:23; 13:28-29). By dying, Jesus set a "new" covenant in motion, a Law written by Him on people's hearts (Jeremiah 31:31-34; Hebrews 10:16).
9. When Jesus comes out of the tomb, those who see Him are frightened at first (Luke 24:37). He is in a transformed state. Yet, even John the apostle who saw Jesus after His resurrection says that he has not seen Jesus in His heavenly state but we all will see Him clearly at His return and will be like Him (I John 3:2).

The connection between the two stories seems unmistakable. This incredible story of Moses that is at the heart of the Exodus event is actually just a foretelling of the greatest story of all time. Not only that, but the detail included in the story goes further than anything we have seen to this point. Consider the story being told in even shorter form:

God instructs His servant to leave His presence and go down to the people who are acting sinfully. God's servant begins to plead that the people not be destroyed and goes down to them. The first law is smashed by God's servant who addresses the poor leadership but gets no reasonable answer—only excuses. The servant tells the people that He will seek the removal of their sin. God forgives the sinful people based upon the relationship He has with the servant. Death is discussed in relationship to seeing God, and the servant is placed in a hole in the rock/ground from which he has a glimpse of God and comes out transformed. He appears before God's people in a transformed state with a new copy of the law written by him at God's direction.

Surely, this is a clear telling of the Jesus story through the greatest leader and prophet in all of Israel's history.

What Did the Apostles Think of the Moses Story?

The Moses story, as we have said, was at the core of everything the Jews were. Even the neighboring Samaritans—though not accepting all the Old Testament scriptures and being despised by the Jews for having allowed non-Jews to become part of their family lines—fully accepted the Torah (first five books of the Old Testament, also known as the book of Moses). Jesus states plainly that Moses wrote about Him and if the leaders of the Jews understood and believed what was written by Moses, they would believe in Him (John 5:46-47).

The New Testament writers have taken Jesus' words very seriously. They understand that everything written about Moses in some way relates to the Jesus story. Whether or not this is true is the really big issue. God sent Moses to rescue his people from bondage and lead them through a time in the wilderness which would be a struggle. But all the people's necessities would be taken care of by God until they reached that great promise land which He gave to them. In the same way, Jesus is sent to rescue God's people from spiritual bondage and guide them through this world of struggle, providing for all necessities, until the time of entering into heaven.

But even on a much more detailed scale, this is true. Peter quotes Deuteronomy 18:15 about *the Prophet* like Moses in Acts 3:22 and applies it directly to Christ before an audience of Jews. Also, Stephen tells the story we have gone over in detail above to accuse the evil Jewish leadership of rejecting Jesus just as their ancestors rejected Moses (Acts 7:37-43), using a quotation of Deuteronomy 18:15, again, to make clear that Jesus is *the Prophet* like Moses that God raised up.

Only through the lens of Jesus can we ever really understand what the story of Moses is about. The Moses story is the Jesus story. It is told in detail in Moses, not just in the big picture sense. Every minor phrase is somehow related to the one and only story that makes sense of everything.

The Tent of Meeting

No doubt you noticed something interesting when you were reading the point-by-point description above. You are probably still interested in a fuller explanation of number 6. There is something so special and powerful here that I just had to save it for the end of the chapter.

Some of you may have noticed when you read through the text earlier that when you came to Exodus 33:7, you started what seemed like a brand new thought. This is not a mistake nor is it simply bad writing. Remember what we said earlier about how the ancient Jewish writer would often write with his most important part in the middle? This is exactly what Moses (by the guidance of God's Spirit) is doing here.

If you will take a moment to read from 33:6 straight to 33:12 you will easily notice that the text flows much better. There is no break. It is as if the story might have easily been written this way and verses 7-11 could have been placed elsewhere so as not to take away from the straight forward sense of the passage. This is quite true. But it is true on purpose. Again, this is not bad writing—it is God's writing, for heaven sake. God did not screw up. Also, the ancients took His Word far too seriously to be haphazard in how they wrote it down. They did not throw little extras in here and there as they came to mind. So what we have here is very intentional.

Actually, I said earlier that the section we are in is really the center section of a very large pattern that begins several chapters back, just after the Ten Commandments are given and elaborated upon. The pattern then goes all the way to the end of Exodus. It is written so that one end of the pattern actually mirrors the other. We will not look at the whole pattern because that is not the goal of this book. But we will say that in this story of Exodus 32-34, we have the middle three pieces of the pattern. The Writer (God, who glories in concealing things by the way—Proverbs 25:2) has taken the story of the writing and giving of the Law to Israel, here in these three chapters, and turned it into two parts.

Before 33:7, we have Moses on the mountain with God while the Law has been written, his making a case for God staying with His people, and his coming down to the people with the Law. After 33:12, we read of Moses on the mountain with God while God dictates and Moses writes the Law, his making a case for God's staying with His people, and his coming down to the people with the Law. It is the same in so many ways. In fact, you can skip from 33:6 straight to 33:12 and not miss a beat. The train of thought goes completely unbroken.

This was a huge clue to the ancient reader. The early, attentive reader looked for very strong similarities or exact opposites in portions of Scripture to indicate where the Author was placing His primary point. In our case, it is not really difficult to discover considering the likeness of the story on either side and the fact that the center (33:7-11) seems to be out of place. It is really just one story pulled apart in the middle, with a piece that is—very precisely—wedged in between.

Now that we see the center clearly, our big question is, "Why?"

Why did God want this little piece of dynamite to be at the heart of this very large section of Exodus? Please read 33:7-11 one more time before we try to give an answer to such a monumental question.

Finished? Good. Here we go.

Staying at the Tent

As we've already alluded to, we have a story in Exodus 32-34 that was basically yanked apart so that this little piece could be placed in the center. It goes without saying that it must be very significant.

This small section is all about the Tent of Meeting. It is an interesting name for this place, but it quickly becomes apparent why it got this name. It is the place where Moses met with God and spoke with God as a man speaks to his friend. Moses was on intimate terms with God in this place.

A person who does not read the Old Testament much and hears of the Tent of Meeting in association with Moses might assume that it was another name for the Tabernacle. But, of course, this is the wrong assumption. The tent is a special place, a unique covering. It is unique, first of all, because it is "outside the camp." Although being inside the camp of God's people was very important because it signified being a sure part of God's chosen people, a "clean" and chosen part, this utterly important place of communication between God and Moses was found only outside the camp. Moses had to leave the camp—and the nearness to the tabernacle—in order to have this intimate connection to God.

Secondly, when Moses goes to the tent, the Israelites are completely attentive. They each watch from the entrance of their own tents and when the pillar of cloud descends at the doorway of the Tent of Meeting (signifying God's presence with Moses) the Israelites then worship, again, from the entrance to their own tents.

Finally, Moses does have to leave the tent. He can't stay there forever, after all. As good as it is to be with God in face-to-face communication, he must return to his duties of governing the people. But there is one who is with him who is going to take his place eventually. He is just a young man. He goes with Moses virtually everywhere. And his name is—get ready—Jesus! That's right. The same name that we read in the New Testament as Jesus is the exact same Hebrew name as Joshua.

So here it is: This brief but incredible snippet taken out of Moses' life is about this savior of Israel who (1) leaves the camp to have the most intimate relationship with God ever experienced by a human; (2) as he is in communication with God this way, all of Israel stands, each by their own tent, and worships [in other words, they do not need to go to the Tabernacle to worship but each can do it from his own living place]; and, (3), there is one who follows in the footsteps of Moses, who will come after him as the leader of Israel and will lead them into the promise land, and who does not "leave the tent," and his name is Jesus/Joshua. Are you kidding me?!

New Testament Connection

The writer of the New Testament book of Hebrews has so much to say about how the ancient Jewish sacrificial system is really just a shadow of Jesus. Every piece of furniture, every sacrifice, and every act of worship was really just another message about Jesus and His once-for-all sacrifice for humankind. It did not escape his notice, either, that there was something God was trying to tell us about Jesus when He insisted that the part of the offerings made to Him be made by burning them outside the camp. The writer drew a connection between those sacrifices and the greatest-of-all sacrifice of Jesus—outside the camp (Hebrews 13:11-13).

When Moses set up the Tent of Meeting outside the camp, it was not a choice of convenience. It was intended to say something about what God was going to do in the Savior. Later, when Christ was killed outside of Jerusalem, it was simply a fulfillment of the fact that the greatest sacrifice to God would be done outside the camp. Like Moses of old, we—through Jesus—go outside the camp to meet God in the most intimate way ever experienced by men.

Another aspect of the story is that the people each worship God at the entrance to their own tents. This also foreshadows what will take place in Jesus.

In the time of Moses, the basic understanding was the true worship of God took place in the tabernacle. But when Jesus is having a conversation with a Samaritan woman in John 4, He makes clear that although the Samaritans believe worship should be offered in one place, and the Jews another, ". . . an hour is coming, and now is, when the true worshipers will worship the Father in Spirit and truth . . ." (John 4:23). Jesus is pointing out that worship isn't in a specific location anymore, but has more to do with the heart than anything else. This relates back to our passage in Exodus because the people are all worshiping from the entrance to their own tents. In other words, they worship from their place of residence—as transient tent-dwellers, foreigners and strangers in the wilderness. They are us. Peter refers to Christians as foreigners and aliens in the world (I Peter 1:1). We wander through this wilderness even now. But, we do all have the gift of being able to worship Christ in Spirit and truth from wherever our wanderings take us. Our worship is not just acceptable when it comes from a specific location such as the temple. Jesus is before God all the time in intimate, personal connection and we offer our worship through Him.

Finally, the passage talks about the next leader in training. Joshua will come after Moses as the great leader of Israel. Joshua, though not a young man when he takes Moses' place to lead the people into the promise land, is referred to as a "young man" in Exodus 33:11. Why tell the reader this? If we really believe every word of Scripture was chosen by God (a premise to which I am fully committed) then there must be a reason for including this detail. It is certainly not necessary in the sentence unless it is alluding to something greater than the immediate story. Who cares if Joshua was young or not, after all? Well . . . we do.

God is telling us that the one who will come after Moses, to lead people in his stead and be a prophet raised up for them like Moses will be a young man. Jesus was only thirty when he began his earthly ministry—just barely old enough to be considered as possibly having something meaningful to contribute to an adult conversation, by ancient Jewish standards. He was very young and yet he was the leader chosen by God to lead the people as Moses, only better.

Also, this is one of the places where we are again told the name of Joshua's father—Nun. A strange sounding name to us, for certain. But again, everything is meaningful. Jesus' name was significant and special for Him and it told of what he would do because it meant "the Lord saves." In our Exodus passage, the author is quick to point out Joshua's dad's name along with Joshua's. Of primary importance to us is what we have already mentioned: Joshua is the exact same Hebrew name as Jesus and the fact that Joshua is the one to historically lead the people into the promise land after Moses has gotten the people right to the brink of entering in is nothing but the biggest clue ever about the coming Messiah. But closely related to that clue is Joshua's dad's name. So get ready. Joshua has the same name as Jesus and his father was named Nun, which means (another drum roll, please) "eternity."

What?! Again—are you kidding?! The name of the one to come after Moses, a prophet like Moses whom God would speak through and to whom the people would listen or die is none other than Jesus, the son of Eternity. Oh yeah, and if that's not enough, we are told in 33:11 that even though Moses had to leave the tent, Joshua/Jesus "would not depart from the tent"!! Hello?! The writer of Hebrews says that Jesus is different from all priests before Him because he always "lives to make intercession" for us. In other words, He never leaves God's presence. The fact that Joshua "would not depart from the tent" is just another incredible indicator of what God intended to do through *THE* Prophet who would come after Moses.

In these few verses, we have seen an incredible picture of the worship that God is ultimately preparing everyone for through Jesus. And, as we've said several times, it is right in the center of the last half of Exodus, which is all about the way to set everything up to offer proper worship to God.

(If you're like me, you may just need to sit where you are for a while and be in awe of the God who wrote this unbelievable Book. Wow. . . Wow, wow, wow.)

Living in the Days of "Joshua"

We are so blessed to be living in the time foretold in the Exodus passage. Unlike the people before Jesus' day, we do not have to anxiously await the time of *the* Prophet. The Prophet has come and has made the throne room of God accessible to every one of us at any time. We live in the time when each one worships God from wherever his tent is staked out and a time when our Savior and Leader never leaves the presence of our Father. Surely, there is no way to express the gratitude we should have in our hearts.

The incredible thing about this passage in Exodus is that it is not just about the ancient Israelites, their leader, and their experience in the wilderness. It is ultimately about Jesus and our experience in worshiping Him. We are the ones who live in tents in a foreign wilderness, who turn our eyes toward Him as he meets with God, and who worship him from any place our feet are planted in this common earthly soil. We are the Israel of God. We have been freed from bondage to worship the one and only true God through *THE* Prophet sent by Him to speak His truth to us.

I love realizing that my tiny little slice of time is caught up in the forever story of God. Don't you?

Chapter 9

Coffee with God

Sometimes when I begin a class nowadays, I ask those who attend to "turn on their Bibles." It generally gets a bit of a laugh.

It still feels strange to live in a time when we have the option of turning on and off our Bibles. So many things can be done electronically. No longer is there a need to think about having a Bible at all times, because as long as we have a cell phone or some electronic device on which we have downloaded the proper app, we can simply tap a touch screen and up pops God's Word. By making a few keystrokes, we can pull up any passage we like, as well as having multiple tools at our command to help us fully understand God's Word. Gone is the day of carrying a three pound Bible under my arm everywhere I go, now the entire Word of God in multiple versions is tucked into my front pocket waiting to satisfy my slightest scriptural craving.

The only problem with this is there is no app to make me crave.

It's great to have the Bible at my fingertips, stored on a chip so small a ladybug could refer to it as a laptop computer, but it hasn't made me more likely to look at it than I was before. I can carry lip balm in my pocket through the west Texas wind all day long and if I never pull it out, my lips still feel like they have been rubbed with hundred-and-fifty-grit sandpaper by the end of the day (claim of experience). I have to use it if I expect it to make a difference.

As you can tell now by reading this book, I love the Word of God. I don't just love it because it has neat things to say and little expressions that give me warm feelings for a few minutes so I can take the next step into my otherwise hectic and horrible day. I love it because it goes so deep and tells me more than I ever would have thought possible about God, Jesus, God's eternal plan, where I fit in the plan, and a thousand aspects of each one of these, just so I don't miss it.

But, again, there is a big flaw in this process: ME. Reading alone—especially just one reading done as quickly as possible to get my daily spiritual quota met—will never be enough. There has to be more to my life than the occasional Bible reading session, which we all have to admit is usually done when the preacher tells us, "Open your Bibles to . . . "

The Bible is the Word of God. Most people in our nation still regard it as a holy book. They believe there is something significant about it that sets it apart on the bookshelf from anything else. Yet most people, by far, even though they have more than one in their home, simply do not open it more than once a month. I believe this is a tragedy. It is one thing to have a Bible yet not claim Christianity as your religion. But it is quite another to take on the name Christian and yet never open God's Word or, God forbid, only open it to make yourself feel better or to make a case for something you already believe to be true. In order to understand God's Word as God intended we will have to get much more serious about understanding it than we have up to this point.

Slam Dunking God's Word

Sometimes, after I've taught a few sessions from a typological way of viewing the Bible, someone will come to me and say that although they absolutely love what they have learned, they will never be able to study the Bible so that they gain similar understandings on their own. The concept of looking at the Bible in a typological way is so foreign to them that they are convinced they will never see any of what God has for His people in His Word from this perspective unless someone shows them. I simply could not disagree more.

Most people in the world will never be able to slam dunk a basketball. That is one of the basic facts of physics. Most of our bodies are not designed in such a way so that, no matter what amount of effort and training we put in, we could soar through the air with a basketball and drive it home by pushing it down into a ten-foot-high goal from above.

But what I cannot believe is that the same principle applies to the truths found in God's Word. Certainly, God has given teachers to the church and it is a special gift that is needed and all parts of the Christian body simply don't have that same gift (Ephesians 4:11). Teachers are good to have around because they are gifted to be able to sift through the Word of God and understand it sometimes a bit more easily than others and they can then pass information along in a way that is both helpful and inspiring to the rest of the body while they are themselves helped and inspired by the worshipers, the servants, the givers, the evangelists, and others. But there is no reason to believe that the truths of Scripture are not available to everyone when the effort to know them is applied with diligence and persistence.

God's Glory is to Conceal

In the last chapter I quoted a part of one of my favorite verses in Scripture. Let's take a better look at it right here. It is Proverbs 25:2:

"It is the glory of God to conceal a matter;
To seek a matter out is the glory of kings."

This is a Scripture we don't spend a lot of time with for various reasons. The main reason is because if it doesn't strike us as particularly good feeling immediately when we read it, we are not likely to pursue the thought further. (Of course, that is assuming we take the time to read it in the first place.) But another reason we don't spend time on a verse like this is because it seems odd when we first start considering what it says.

Just think about it for a second—"It is the glory of God to conceal a matter . . ."? Hmmm. Really? God's glory is to *conceal*? That's strange. We don't think of God as concealing things. We might think, *I thought God was a good God who liked to give people stuff for free. It doesn't sound like what I have heard before about God that He would try to hide something. Isn't that against God's character?*

But, actually, this is not at all foreign to what we know about God. In Job, God never answers Job's questions about why he is suffering so badly. Obviously, God has the answer but He is not going to tell Job because the lesson for Job is to learn to *trust* God even though he doesn't know all that is going on behind the scenes.

Again, in Matthew 11:25, Jesus praises God for having hidden certain things from the wise and understanding and having revealed them to babes. Obviously, there is a distinction between those who get to know the great truths of God and those who do not and it is God who decides when truth is revealed. It is not because one is smart enough to have earned the knowledge. It is because God chooses to reveal it. And to whom does he reveal it?

For a good answer, let's turn again to Psalm 119. This is the longest chapter in all of Scripture. It is an incredible poem about the perfection of God's Word. That is its one huge point. I cannot help but find it appropriate in every way that the longest chapter of the Bible just happens to be about how *great* the Word of God is. And in 119:18 we read the psalmist's plea to God, "Open my eyes that I may see wonderful things in your Law." Clearly, the psalmist knows there are fantastic truths "hidden" in God's Word that only God can give him the eyes to see. It is not his diligence that will allow him to uncover such concealed mysteries. It is God's favor on him.

It is not the author's desire to force God to give him the secrets of His Word by earning them through devoted study. He will show God his heart that longs with all of his being to know God's Word fully and it is because of his desire to truly *know* God that God will answer. God doesn't hand out the secrets of the Kingdom of heaven to those who don't even care for them. It is our passion to know them and our relentless pursuit of them that proves our hearts, and God has always been most concerned with the heart.

I believe that God wishes for us to approach His Word this way. He wishes for us to devote ourselves to it, to pray to Him over it, and to trust that He will give us the eyes to see the wonderful secrets that He has concealed throughout its pages.

Seeing Jesus

Seeing the Christ-story throughout Scripture is a gift available to everyone. But what it will require from us is commitment. It is always wonderful to see the Jesus-story in the Bible in a place where you had not before, even when shown by someone else—a brother or sister in Christ who is as in love with God's Word as you. But the joy is enhanced twenty-fold when we see it through our own time and devotion to meeting God in His Word and He opens some door that was previously shut to us but is suddenly flung wide open so that the story of Jesus hits us full on, somewhere we had never imagined it to be but where now it is plainly displayed on center stage. What an incredible moment of excitement it is to meet God in this way. We truly come into contact with the Father as He, Himself, leads us by His Spirit through His inspired Word. Not only do I believe this is possible, I believe it is something for which we are all encouraged to strive.

But how?

There are some principles which can be applied to Bible study in order to strengthen our walk with God through this avenue of seeing the Christ-story in His Word. Let's take a closer look at these principles and get a better idea of just how to start on this path of submitting to the transformation of our minds so that we see the Jesus story in all the clarity that God intended.

1. Know Jesus' Story

The first among the necessary aspects of Jesus-centered Bible study is to know the Jesus story inside and out. It sounds elementary. But not to say it would be almost criminal and would leave the impression that it is alright to know just the very basics. That will never be enough.

Jesus is the key to the Christian faith. Exactly four books in the Bible are devoted to giving us the most important, most necessary aspects of the Jesus story for all of His followers to know. Only with our complete devotion to these four books—Matthew, Mark, Luke, and John—will we be able to see many of the clues throughout Scripture that will lead us closer to a full view of the Christ story in many of the places where it would otherwise go unnoticed. There is no substitute for knowing the Christ story from start to finish.

For instance, when we went through the story of Daniel in the lions' den in chapter 2, we saw the connection between the fact that just as the stone on the entrance to the den was sealed with the king's ring after Daniel was thrown in, so was the stone over Jesus' tomb sealed insuring that no one would tamper with the body at the threat of death. Of course, it does not make or break the connection to the Jesus story. But it is just another of the details that is used by God to show what will happen to the Messiah in the events surrounding His death centuries in the future. Together, the many details paint an undeniable picture of God's plan in Jesus.

2. Meditation

Nineteenth century preacher Charles Spurgeon once said, "Some people like to read so many chapters every day. I would not dissuade them from the practice, but I would rather lay my soul asoak in half a dozen verses all day than rinse my hand in several chapters. Oh, to be bathed in a text of Scripture, and to let it be sucked up in your very soul, till it saturates your heart!"

This quote sums up my feelings about the very best way to study God's Word. We are a culture of doers and that does not generally lead to good Bible study. The best of Bible study is in the consideration, the mulling over, the reading time and time again until the verses that make up a passage are all but completely memorized so that they fill the mind in every moment of mental relaxation. To meditate is to think about in the fullest manner possible. God meets His people through this spiritual discipline.

Returning to Psalm 119:148, we see that the writer would rather meditate on God's Word than sleep. Can we honestly say that if we were forced to choose between the two in the middle of the night we would rather meditate on the Bible? I'm not saying anyone is unspiritual for wanting to sleep in. In my house, we treat the enjoyment of a good nap as a positive character trait. But there is no doubt that a devotion to meditating on God's Word, even above what might be considered some of the most desirable parts of life, would be beneficial to all of us.

3. Longsuffering (nicely referred to as Patience)

This is closely linked to the idea of meditation. Yet it deserves its own entry because meditation is not, by itself, a necessarily long process. Generally speaking, however, it is in the process of meditation that insights about how to understand a certain passage are received. This process will, at times, last for a long period. This is where longsuffering comes in. It is by no means a "suffering" process to study God's Word (although I suppose there are those that think of it this way because of bad spiritual leadership or a rough past experience). Longsuffering has to do with sticking with it. It refers to tenacity and the willingness to submit to God's timing. We enter into God's Word with a commitment to wait as long as necessary for God to bring full understanding to us.

This does not mean that we should not read or listen to what others have to say on a passage or a subject. But it does mean that we are constantly before God, in listening prayer and two-way conversation, waiting until He brings the insight that will give the clarity that is valuable and meaningful to our current walk of faith. In this process, our minds are renewed (Romans 12:2).

Psalm 25:4-5 says, "Make me know your ways, O Lord; teach me your paths. Lead me in your truth and teach me, for you are the God of my salvation; for you I wait all the day long." The author wants God to be the teacher that leads him to truth and he is committed to waiting on the Lord as long as it takes. We should have the same devotion to staying put before God until He has made the way before us clear. In our Bible study, we should be completely humbled before Him, waiting for His guidance and His opening of our minds before moving on to something easier or to something that we already feel we understand and so do not need further direction (which, of course, is always false no matter how fully memorized a passage may be).

When I was first learning to study the Word of God—not just read what scholars say about a passage, but really submit to God—I was preaching through the Gospel of Mark. I started seeing what I could only identify as an incredible use of literary structure. But although I searched through all the commentaries and encyclopedias I could find, I could not locate anyone saying anything about what I was seeing. I was certain that the structure was there and was definitely big enough to receive at least some kind of mention. Yet it received none. Eventually, I tucked the information away in some corner of my mind but returned to it from time to time over several years, occasionally gaining new understandings as God opened my mind further.

Finally, God brought me into contact with a brother in Christ who lived hundreds of miles away from me but who had spent years in a similar personal study of the Book of Matthew. Obviously, there was some amount of overlap in our insights. But we also shared a connection in being convinced that more was in the gospels we studied than we were able to completely back up with information from outside sources. This meeting and the friendship that developed fanned the flame of my sporadic study in Mark into a full blown bonfire. Over several months, the depth to which God took me was remarkable as I drank deeply from God's well concerning the makeup and richness of Mark's Gospel. God didn't tell me when the world was going to end or give me some secret code for interpretation. But the Word came alive to me as never before and it was just Him, me, His Word, and the occasional outside source to which He led me. Most of the insights He gave me were just through the use of the Bible, a concordance, and a whole lot of waiting.

I learned to be still during that time and simply let God open my eyes as I did my part by immersing myself in His Word. I now consider longsuffering/patience/waiting for God to be one of the most indispensible parts of solid Bible study.

4. Interpret Consistently

When studying with typology in mind and trying to view the Scriptures in light of Jesus, as the apostles who wrote the New Testament certainly did, it is very important to remain consistent in how one understands symbols throughout the Bible. We need to be careful not to make connections that cannot be maintained throughout Scripture. This simply means that "vineyard/vine" should be interpreted similarly throughout our Bible study. It will not always have the exact same reference point, but there will be very close connections in how it should be understood from passage to passage.

For instance, we see the vineyard referred to in Isaiah 5:1-7. It is a passage that makes completely clear in 5:7 that the vineyard is Israel, itself. If we watch closely throughout Scripture we can see that vineyards and vines are often used symbolically to refer to Israel. But they can also simply be used as a reference to the good or bad of another nation. However, it is primarily Israel that is represented. This is again the case in Psalm 80:8. I Kings 4:25 speaks of how a sign of Israel and Judah's prosperity is that each person is under his own vine and fig tree. It is a way of saying everyone is doing well. If Israel does well, the vine produces well. As goes Israel, so goes the produce of the vine. Isaiah 24:7 associates the withering of the vine with the judgment that is coming upon Israel.

Now fast forward to John 15:1 where Jesus begins a talk with the disciples about how He is the "true vine." This is Jesus' way of telling the disciples that as Israel was first established to be used as God's chosen servant but proved their unfaithfulness and inability over the centuries, it is now Jesus who represents the true Israel, the Servant that will live up completely to all the Father's expectations. All those who wish to know the Father and be a part of His people must be connected to Christ (15:4). The ancient Jews would have said that the only way to become a part of God's chosen people was to become a Jew. As "vine" throughout the Old Testament symbolizes nations and especially the nation of Israel, so in the New Testament, it keeps the same symbolism. Namely, the group of people caught up in Christ form the one people of God under the one King, Jesus. And that vine will always grow with bountiful fruit.

In Bible study, we seek to keep our understanding of symbols consistent. Even though we cannot always tell what meaning is related to a particular symbol, it is important that we interpret with a meaning that takes into account the variety of contexts in which a word is found throughout the Bible. This keeps meaning more accurate. There are various resources that can help us with understanding several symbols in Scripture. However, I found none to be of such quality that I would highly recommend them. All do well with some symbols, but many—even most meanings given to most symbols—are only partial. The whole of Scripture is not taken into account. Once again, the best way to understand any part of Scripture will be not to run to study helps too quickly. Meditation on Scripture (two-way conversation with God over His Word) in "longsuffering" diligence will always yield the best result. God may give you the answer through a study aid but it should be because it was His way of showing you the answer, not your way of attempting to side-step the study process.

5. Order

Finally, if you are going to interpret the Scriptures typologically, there must be order to your interpretation. The most important story in all of history is told in our sacred Book. God has not thrown it in willy-nilly so that our methods for drawing conclusions about the meaning of the Bible would be made fun of by the thoughtful investigator. I am not talking about the person who is already dead set against the Christian faith or even the person who simply gives the subject no thought at all. I am talking about the person who comes with serious questions and would like solid answers that have true thought and meaning behind them.

To call someone a "Christian intellectual" has been considered an oxymoron for some time by many people throughout the world. Although some have taken this stance regarding our teaching without having given proper thought to what we believe, others view us this way because they have seen poor application of the mental ability we have as we should use it to understand God's Word. God gave us our minds and He is even in the business of renewing them, as I said earlier (Romans 12:2). Our thoughts should be well-grounded and our application of Scripture should be provocative and reasonable to the truly curious seeker.

This means that when we approach Scripture, we do not rush to shove our thoughts—even our thoughts about where the death and resurrection of Christ might fit—into every random passage. Using symbols and understandings gained through weeks, months, and even years of devotion and attention to the Word of God and the Spirit's lead, we present a case that can be followed by the curious seeker and can be grasped by the intellectually open listener. This is exactly what Stephen does in Acts 7 and Paul in Acts 13. They meet the thinkers where they are and speak to them in a way that is consistent, meaningful, and orderly, and makes Christ the focal point of the Old Testament text.

For example, the Jonah story which we talked about earlier is not a bunch of thrown-together bits and pieces which randomly coincide with different parts of Israel's history and Christ's earthly ministry. It is the story of Israel's unwillingness to be a light to the Gentiles throughout history leading up to the death of Christ and his completely unexpected resurrection followed by the taking of the message of salvation to the Gentile world, using a Savior birthed out of Israel even though the nation, as a whole, remained reluctant to take part in the plan of God. The Book of Jonah tells one orderly story throughout. That is not to say that each character in Scripture tells the story of Jesus in their life just one time, which is certainly not the case. But no matter what is being told, there will be a consistent and well-structured presentation when all the pieces are understood. This is what will give our explanation the credibility that a Book written by the One and only God of the universe deserves.

A Pillar of Faith

No one is a master of symbols like the author of Revelation. (Yes, the Holy Spirit is the true Author, of course, and the greatest Master of all writing styles.) Revelation is full of symbols from front to back. There is virtually nothing included in the book, even in the first three chapters—which involve an introduction of Jesus in the form of a warrior and the letters to seven churches— that is not presented through the use of symbols. In the message to Philadelphia, the sixth church named in the book, Jesus has nothing to say about any bad behavior or lack of faith in the church. Ultimately, for those who overcome, Jesus promises to make them a "pillar in the temple of my God" (Revelation 3:12).

There can hardly be a doubt that this symbol involves steadfastness of faith. Their "endurance" has already been praised in 3:8 where they are said to have been faithful and true to the name of Christ. For those who remain true to Christ through the persecution they endure, there awaits the honor of being made a pillar in God's temple. In other words, it is the kind of faith that gives strength to the temple of God—His Church. It holds up the temple and is something that provides stability to the whole. A wonderful image.

This is something to which we should all aspire. We want to be pillars of faith. We wish to be the kind of people upon which the temple of God can rely and that keep it standing strong. We are the people of God and we stand because it is God who gives us the strength to stand firm in Him. He has the power to make us the pillars in His house.

One of the ways that we become those pillars is by our reliance upon His Word. We trust that we can spiritually survive whatever may come because His Word assures us that we will as we grow in Him. And we trust His Word because we are confident He wrote it. But our confidence will rarely be enough to help the person who is sincerely seeking truth and investigating Christianity come to a point of thoughtful consideration of our message that Jesus really is the only Way, Truth, and Life.

Typology Strengthens Faith

Ultimately, our faith should rest on our true personal connection to the Lord, Himself. We come into contact with Him and converse with Him and He leads and guides us directly and intimately. But I could hardly say that I rest in nothing but my own personal and intimate connection to Him to be a hundred percent certain of everything I know about Him. I wish I could say this was so, but sadly it is not. I am sure there are many others who love Jesus more than anything in the world, yet still find themselves somewhat battered in the fight against the forces of evil that seem to strike ceaselessly against the faith we hold so dear. If you sometimes wonder what it is that makes your Christian faith so different from any other faith I have two things to say to you: (1) You are not alone; and (2) your faith can be immeasurably strengthened by a better knowledge of typology and how to see the Scriptures with Jesus as the lens you use to look at everything.

In recent years, when I have found my faith most assaulted, I have discovered that it is virtually unshakable as I recall what I have learned through my study of typology. I cannot think of anything that comes close to giving me the least bit of insecurity over the truth of God's Word when I consider what is said about Jesus in the Old Testament types.

We mentioned earlier that most scholars now admit that the Old Testament texts reached their final form no later than a hundred years before Jesus laid in a manger in Bethlehem. This is undeniable, in large part, because of the discovery of the Dead Sea Scrolls (see chapter 6). Every book of the Old Testament (except Esther) was at least partially represented in this discovery that dates from approximately 100 B.C. to 50 A.D. For this to be the case, they would have to be well-established in their form before that time. Obviously, we didn't discover the original texts of the Old Testament. They were widely circulated long before the copies that were discovered were first hidden in caves in the face of the Roman devastation of Jerusalem in A.D. 70. And we have not even begun to talk about the Greek translation of the Hebrew text which also has a date of origin long before Christ's birth.

What all of this means is that the Word of God that we now call the Old Testament was around for a very long time before Jesus' earthly life ever began. The story of Jesus—including being sent by His Father, His place of birth, His ministry, His followers coming primarily from society's outcasts, the plots to kill Him, the feeding of multitudes, the rejection and ridicule, His seamless robe, His thorny crown, His death on a cross, His day of death, His burial in an unused tomb, His resurrection on the third day, His transformed appearance to the disciples, the taking of the message of Jesus to the Gentiles, and almost countless other details—was told long before it ever took place. The fact that this great Story—the One and Only Story—is told over and over and over again throughout God's Word is testimony to Jesus being the One at the center of God's plan all along.

This is why the disciples could argue so convincingly from the Scriptures that Jesus was the Christ. It is also why it made so much sense for Paul to begin his evangelism by teaching in the synagogues of every new town he entered. As Jesus Himself said, He was the One about whom the Scriptures spoke (John 5:39). The types give our faith a certainty that God intended and make the arrows of Satan much less effective.

Ada Habershon, a great teacher of typology, wrote the following over a hundred years ago: "Many are giving up the simple truths of God's Word. The inspiration of the Scriptures is attacked on all sides; the doctrine of the atonement is denied, or thought little of; whilst other things are preached which are contrary to the Word. This could not be so frequently the case if the Old Testament types were more carefully studied and more widely taught."[7]

I could not agree more.

When God Has You Over for Coffee

The types in the Old Testament link the entire Word of God together in perfect harmony. When we see just how deep the river of the Christ story runs throughout God's Word, from Genesis to Revelation, we have an assurance that starts in our minds and works its way deep into our hearts. Jesus is the key to understanding all of God's Word and everything leads up to His ministry and sacrifice. Once we become aware of just how true this is, we greatly increase our ability to discern meaning from God's Word and to steadfastly withstand the world's assault on our faith.

If we have ever wondered where our allegiance should lie or if the Word of God is really different than any other book in existence, typology makes clear that the follower of Jesus has a foundation for faith greater than that offered by any other religion. Because the story of Jesus was told in such great detail so many times and so long before He set foot on the earth, we can be certain that the God of the Bible is the only God to whom our hearts belong.

I love my God. I love my Savior, Jesus. And I love the Word of God. With complete humility I would say that sometimes I feel I could almost write Psalm 119 myself. Like Moses speaking with God face-to-face as a man speaks with his friend, I often find myself in what I can only describe as a similar relationship. I do not see God, of course. But I am caught up with Him in conversation through His Word in a way that I never experience in any other setting. For me, Bible study is so tightly united with prayer that I can hardly separate the two. He shows me His will, sometimes broadly and sometimes very specifically. I do not feel the same kind of intimacy every time but there is often a connection that is made between God and me that is as real and true as me sharing life over coffee with an old friend. These are the moments I long for in my study, and they are the moments I believe God wishes for all of us.

    I encourage you not to miss out on this relationship for yourself. Learn to meet Him in His Word. Ask for His presence and His intimacy with you. Ask for Him to change you and make you more like His Son through the communion you share in His Word. Stop seeing the Bible as just a book. See it as the door on which you knock and which He will always be there to open so you can enter a place where the coffee is fresh and the conversation is life-changing.

Endnotes

[1] Patrick Fairbairn, *Typology of Scripture* (Grand Rapids, MI: Kregel Publications, 1989), 20.

[2] Augustine, *Quaestiones in Heptateuchum,* 2.73.

[3] Augustine, *City of God*, 16.2.

[4] Philip S. Watson, *Let God Be God!: An Interpretation of the Theology of Martin Luther* (Philadelphia, PA: Wipf & Stock Publishers, 2001), 149.

[5] G. R. Osborne, "Hermeneutics," in *Dictionary of the Later New Testament* (Downers Grove, IL: IVP Academic, 1997), 479.

[6] Richard Soulen, *Sacred Scripture: A Short History of Interpretation* (Louisville, KY: Westminster John Knox Press, 2010), 62.

[7] Ada Habershon, *Study of the Types* (Grand Rapids, MI: Kregel Publications, 1974), 10.

Printed in Great Britain
by Amazon